Philippians
Colossians
Philemon

The People's Bible

ROLAND CAP EHLKE
General Editor

ARMIN J. PANNING
New Testament Editor

G. JEROME ALBRECHT
Manuscript Editor

Philippians Colossians Philemon

HARLYN J. KUSCHEL

NORTHWESTERN PUBLISHING HOUSE
Milwaukee, Wisconsin

The cover and interior illustrations were originally executed by James Tissot (1836-1902). The maps of Paul's journeys were drawn by Dr. John Lawrenz, Saginaw, Michigan.

Scripture taken from the HOLY BIBLE, NEW INTERNATIONAL VERSION. Copyright © 1973, 1978, 1984 International Bible Society. Used by permission of Zondervan Bible Publishers.

Library of Congress Card 86-60431
Northwestern Publishing House
1250 N. 113th St., P.O. Box 26975, Milwaukee, WI 53226-0975
© 1986 by Northwestern Publishing House.
Published 1986
Printed in the United States of America
ISBN 0-8100-0241-8

CONTENTS

Paul

Painting by James Tissot

EDITOR'S PREFACE

The People's Bible is just what the name implies — a Bible for the people. It includes the complete text of the Holy Scriptures in the popular New International Version. The commentary following the Scripture sections contains personal applications as well as historical background and explanations of the text.

The authors of *The People's Bible* are men of scholarship and practical insight, gained from years of experience in the teaching and preaching ministries. They have tried to avoid the technical jargon which limits so many commentary series to professional Bible scholars.

The most important feature of these books is that they are Christ-centered. Speaking of the Old Testament Scriptures, Jesus himself declared, "These are the Scriptures that testify about me" (John 5:39). Each volume of *The People's Bible* directs our attention to Jesus Christ. He is the center of the entire Bible. He is our only Savior.

The commentaries also have maps, illustrations and archaeological information when appropriate. All the books include running heads to direct the reader to the passage he is looking for.

This commentary series was initiated by the Commission on Christian Literature of the Wisconsin Evangelical Lutheran Synod.

It is our prayer that this endeavor may continue as it began. We dedicate these volumes to the glory of God and to the good of his people.

Roland Cap Ehlke

GENERAL INTRODUCTION TO
THE PRISON EPISTLES

Philippians, Colossians and Philemon, together with Ephesians, form a group of the Apostle Paul's epistles collectively designated as the "prison epistles" or "captivity letters." Paul writes all four epistles while in prison. He speaks of his bonds and his unique calling as the Lord's "ambassador in chains." These common expressions, the similarity of the various personal remarks the apostle makes in all four epistles, and the fact that three of the four were delivered to their destinations by one man, Tychicus, lead us to the conclusion that all four of these letters were written during the same period of confinement.

Paul was imprisoned in Rome. He was awaiting the hearing of his appeal to the emperor and then the emperor's verdict. This was probably a period of about two years, from A.D. 61 to 63. This particular imprisonment is sometimes referred to as Paul's first Roman imprisonment. He was also imprisoned in Rome a second time, just before his death.

In Acts 21-27 St. Luke tells in great detail how it happened that Paul appealed to the emperor and consequently journeyed to Rome for the hearing. Because these events have a direct bearing on all three epistles, it is worthwhile to review some of them here.

During the apostle's mission journeys Jews in various places resisted and rejected the gospel message. On occasion

1

this resistance became violent. Many of these unbelieving Jews brought false reports concerning Paul and his gospel proclamation back to Jerusalem. They stirred up the resentment of their fellow Jews by accusing Paul of teaching the Jews to turn away from Moses and encouraging them not to circumcise their children or live according to Jewish customs.

This smoldering Jewish resentment was fanned into flame when Paul returned to Jerusalem after his third mission journey and appeared in the temple. There a group of Asian Jews incited a riot by publicly accusing Paul of forsaking the law of Moses and polluting the temple by bringing a Gentile into the area of the temple reserved exclusively for Jews. The charges were false, but they were enough to arouse the whole anti-Christian element in Jerusalem. Paul would doubtless have been stoned to death on the spot had not the Roman garrison commander intervened and brought a detachment of soldiers to stem the murderous fury of the mob.

When an attempt by the apostle to defend himself before his Jewish accusers resulted in another near riot, the commander detained Paul. Hoping to have the charges against the apostle clarified, he called an informal meeting of the Jewish Council (Sanhedrin), but that meeting, too, degenerated into a shouting match. Meanwhile, Paul assured himself of humane treatment by informing the commander that he was a Roman citizen. When a plot on the apostle's life was discovered, the commander decided to have Paul removed to the seat of the imperial government at Caesarea.

With his arrival at Caesarea Paul began an almost five-year period of unjust and unwarranted captivity, hearings and appeals. It must have been a difficult and discouraging time for the apostle, but Paul did not lose heart. He continued to glorify Christ in his chains and even by means of them. It was during these years that the apostle could optimistically write, "I have learned to be content whatever the circumstances" (Philippians 4:11).

The first two years of Paul's imprisonment took place in Caesarea under the weak but vicious procurator Felix. Shortly after the apostle's arrival in Caesarea his enemies appeared. They accused him of being a "troublemaker, stirring up riots among the Jews all over the world . . . and desecrating the temple," but Paul eloquently defended himself against the charges. Felix, however, did not release Paul, probably because he feared the Jews. He also hoped for a bribe from the apostle.

When Festus replaced Felix as governor, the Jewish leaders renewed their accusations against Paul. Again, no charges worthy of imprisonment could be proven, but Festus, too, wanted to maintain the favor of the Jews. So he suggested that Paul go to Jerusalem and stand trial there. By this time Paul was convinced that he could never receive a fair trial in either Jerusalem or Caesarea. So Paul exercised the right that every Roman citizen had and appealed his case directly to the emperor, secure in the Lord's assurance that he would testify of Jesus also in Rome. Festus, somewhat unwillingly, granted the appeal. And events were set in motion which brought the apostle to Rome. Acts 27 and 28 describe Paul's long and perilous journey to Rome.

At Rome the appeal process dragged on for over two years. All the while Paul was considered a prisoner. The terms of his imprisonment, however, were quite lenient. Though he was continually fastened to a soldier/guard with a light chain, the apostle was permitted to carry on a fairly

3

normal schedule of activity. He lived in his own rented dwelling in Rome. He received his friends and co-workers, including Timothy, Tychicus, Luke, Epaphroditus and others, without hindrance and sent them on various errands to extend his ministry.

In general he continued to proclaim the gospel joyfully and vigorously to all with whom he came in contact. The preaching and the attitude of the Lord's "ambassador in chains" encouraged the Christians who were already at Rome and resulted in the conversion of members of the Praetorian guard and members of Caesar's household.

At the conclusion of the Book of Acts we find Paul preaching and teaching the gospel quite openly in Rome. How wonderfully the Lord fulfilled his promise that Paul would testify of him in the foremost city of the first-century world.

We don't know why Paul's hearing was delayed so long in Rome. No doubt Roman jurisprudence, like our own, was somewhat cumbersome. Perhaps the apostle's opponents despaired of obtaining his condemnation and resorted to delaying tactics, as desperate lawyers often do today. Or perhaps the whole matter of the free teaching of an "Oriental religion" by a Roman citizen had to be thoroughly investigated by the emperor's advisors.

In his epistle to the Philippians, which we take to be the last of these four captivity epistles, the apostle informs us that his first hearing has taken place and that it has gone well. Though he does not foolishly ignore the possibility that the emperor might still rule against him, Paul is optimistic that he will be acquitted and set free.

Based on what the apostle says in Philippians, most Bible scholars assume that Paul was set free and continued to work until he was imprisoned again in the general persecution of Christians that took place under Emperor Nero in A.D. 65-66. During this second imprisonment Paul wrote 2 Timothy, which is clearly the last testimony of a man facing his earthly end.

Paul did not lose heart during his years as a prisoner, for he realized that his imprisonment, with all its attendant frustrations and inconveniences, was an essential and fruitful part of his ministry for Christ. In the captivity letters the apostle speaks of his own sufferings as an extension of Christ's sufferings, borne for the sake of Christ's church. He regarded his hearing before the imperial court as an opportunity to witness for the defense and confirmation of the gospel.

Yes, his sufferings remained sufferings, and he felt them keenly, but Paul knew that even these sufferings were part of the grace bestowed on him in his ministry. His immediate purpose in being in Rome was to appeal to Caesar, but his higher objective was to continue to proclaim the gospel. This he did, to the Jews and to the Gentiles, ever hopeful and energetic, "boldly and without hindrance . . . preaching the kingdom of God and . . . the Lord Jesus Christ."

The most far-reaching fruits of the apostle's ministry in chains are his captivity letters. From the inspired pen of the Lord's captive ambassador the church has received a wonderful proclamation of the all-embracing significance of Christ (Colossians), a testimony of how the gospel can transfigure even the darkest aspects of human life (Philemon), a remarkable portrait of the nature of the church (Ephesians), and a letter whose dominant note of hope and joy even in the midst of discouragement and suffering (Philippians) has kept the church of every age optimistic and hopeful.

Philippians is probably the last of Paul's captivity letters. When Paul wrote Colossians and Philemon, Luke and Aristarchus were still with him. When Philippians was written, both had been sent out on apostolic missions. Philippians also contains the latest information we have on the progress of Paul's appeal and implies that the final verdict could be expected at any time.

We conclude, therefore, that all four of the prison epistles were written during Paul's first imprisonment in Rome during the years A.D. 61-63. Colossians was probably written first, followed by Philemon, Ephesians and finally Philippians. The church has always accepted these letters as authentic messages from the hand of the Apostle Paul, the Lord's inspired "ambassador in chains."

PHILIPPIANS
INTRODUCTION

The first of the three captivity letters we shall consider in this volume was actually the last one written. Paul addressed it to the "the saints of Jesus Christ at Philippi." At the time the apostle wrote this letter, Philippi was still a rather important city. It had a long and eventful history. When Philip II, the father of Alexander the Great, began to expand the Macedonian empire shortly after he seized the throne in 359 B.C., he quickly annexed the territory in which the city called Krenides, meaning "fountains," was located. He enlarged and fortified the city, then named it Philippi, after himself.

For many years the riches extracted from the gold mines around Philippi helped both Philip and Alexander maintain their armies and enlarge their kingdom. Their conquests brought Hellenistic culture and the Greek language to the entire Mediterranean world and, according to God's divine plan, paved the way for the preaching of the gospel in the entire area. If Philip and Alexander had not extended their empire to the east, the Apostle Paul and the gospel could not have later moved so rapidly west.

The Romans conquered the old Macedonian empire some two hundred years after its founding by Philip. By that time the gold mines around Philippi were exhausted, and the city had become a ghost town. But subsequent events made Philippi an important city again, this time in the Roman empire. In 42 B.C. Philippi was the site of the battle in which Brutus and Cassius, who had led the plot to assassinate Julius Caesar, were defeated by Mark Antony and Octavian, who later became Caesar Augustus.

Soon after that battle Philippi was made a Roman colony, and Mark Antony settled some of his veterans there. After Augustus became sole ruler of the empire in 31 B.C., he continued the policy of settling retired veterans in Philippi. In Paul's day Philippi was the leading city of one of the four political regions of the old Macedonian empire. The fact that the Egnatian Way, the main road from Rome to Asia, ran through Philippi also made the city strategically important to the empire.

The policy of designating certain key cities throughout the vast Roman empire as colonies and settling veterans and their families there was advantageous to both the veterans and the empire. The veterans were rewarded for their service to the empire with land grants and special political privileges, and the empire had loyal Roman citizens situated at strategic points throughout its conquered territories.

As a Roman colony Philippi was a Rome in miniature, a little bit of Italy on foreign soil. Its inhabitants were primarily Roman. The few natives that remained after the Roman conquest gradually coalesced with the Roman settlers. Like all the colonists throughout the empire, the Philippians took great pride in being Roman. They dressed as Romans, used Roman coins and maintained Latin as the offical language of their city. Realizing this helps us understand how quickly the Philippian townspeople could be stirred up by charges that Paul and his companions were "Jews . . . advocating customs unlawful for us Romans to accept and practice" (Acts 16:20).

It also casts light on many of the references and expressions Paul uses in his epistle to the Philippians. Families of Roman veterans would surely identify with the Praetorian

8

guard and Caesar's household. The lesson on Christians' heavenly citizenship would be particularly meaningful to those who were so proud of their earthly citizenship. And Christians who were no doubt constantly pressured to worship the emperor and persecuted when they refused needed to be reminded of the greatness of the glorified Christ and encouraged in their loyalty to him.

Philippi was located at the extreme northern end of the Aegean Sea in what is now Greece. Like many ancient cities it was situated on a hill overlooking a plain. The Gangites River, along which the small Jewish community in Paul's day met for prayer, was located about a mile east of the city. After receiving his "Macedonian call" at Troas, Paul took a ship to Neapolis. Then he traveled by foot on the Egnatian Way to Philippi, and there he founded the first Christian congregation on the continent of Europe.

In Acts 16 Luke tells us of Paul's first visit to Philippi and the founding of the congregation there. This took place during Paul's second missionary journey. From the first Sabbath contact with a little group of women who met for prayer along the river to God's dramatic deliverance of Paul and Silas from prison at midnight, there is high drama and wonderful evidence of the Lord's hand controlling the movement of the gospel westward from Jerusalem to Rome. We suggest the reading of Acts 16 as background before the reader studies the epistle to the Philippians in detail.

From Philippi Paul and Silas continued on to Thessalonica. Timothy, who was also in the apostle's party, remained behind briefly in Philippi before joining the apostle again. Luke remained longer in Philippi to provide spiritual leadership for the young congregation.

On his third missionary journey Paul visited Philippi twice, both as he was outward bound and as he was home-

9

ward bound. The last stop was brief and unplanned. Paul had wanted to sail from Corinth to Syria, but the discovery of a plot against his life by hostile Jews persuaded him to retrace his route through Macedonia toward Asia. It was on this return journey that Luke again rejoined the apostle.

The extraordinary experiences the apostle and the members of the congregation had shared, as well as the eager, generous faith of Philippian believers like Lydia, the converted jailer and others, resulted in a special relationship between the congregation at Philippi and the Apostle Paul. The Philippians sent gifts to help the apostle and support his work on several occasions. During Paul's imprisonment in Rome they even sent one of their own members, Epaphroditus, to deliver a gift to the apostle and to remain with him to assist him. The Philippians were very concerned about the apostle's welfare during his confinement in Rome and eager to know of the outcome of his trial before the imperial court.

Unlike Romans or Colossians or other of his epistles which center on great doctrinal themes, Paul's epistle to the Philippians is in many ways an inspired friendly letter. It passes easily from one subject to another, as our own letters generally tend to do. Much of what the apostle writes in his epistle to the Philippians was prompted by the visit of Epaphroditus to Rome. The Philippians' gesture of love in sending him both a gift and a helper touched the apostle deeply. No doubt he acknowledged their goodness at once, perhaps through someone traveling back to Philippi soon after Epaphroditus arrived in Rome. In this epistle, however, Paul makes grateful, written acknowledgement of the Philippians' generosity, which has served to greatly increase his joy.

Epaphroditus, naturally, brought the apostle a report about conditions in the Philippian congregation. The report was generally good. The Philippian Christians were adorning their Christian confession with lives that honored the Lord. They were giving constant evidence of a loving and generous spirit. They were ready to suffer if need be for the sake of Christ. The congregation had grown and seems at the time to have been untroubled by doctrinal controversy or severe persecution.

Yet there were certain areas in which the congregation at Philippi, like every Christian congregation, needed encouragement. With great tact Paul urges all the members to strive for greater harmony and humility in Christ. He warns them against some of the spiritual dangers that surround them. He makes a personal plea to two of the congregation's women, Euodia and Syntyche, to settle their differences in a God-pleasing way. And he includes many practical suggestions for growing in faith and in Christian living.

Because they were deeply concerned about their beloved apostle's welfare, the Philippians were eager for a report about the apostle's personal well-being and the progress of his trial. Early in the epistle Paul provides us with the most detailed information we have about both.

Epaphroditus, who had been sent to Paul by the Philippians to serve the apostle's needs, had worked so diligently at his task that he had become gravely ill. After he had recovered from his near-fatal illness, the apostle thought it best to send him back home to Philippi. No doubt Epaphroditus was disappointed that he had not been able to stay longer with the apostle. Perhaps he wondered how the believers back home would receive him if he returned sooner than they expected. Paul, too, was concerned. In this epistle, which Epaphroditus carried back to Philippi, the apostle

11

explained the circumstances of his faithful servant's return and encouraged the Philippians to lovingly receive him and honor him for the work he had done.

In the 104 verses of his epistle to the Philippians we can observe many sides of the Apostle Paul's personality. We see him as a joyful servant of Christ, an optimistic prisoner, a humble cross-bearer, a thoughtful administrator, an untiring idealist, a tactful pastor and a grateful friend, but the epistle's primary focus is not on the man Paul. It is on the Lord Jesus, whose grace made the apostle everything he was.

The thread that holds together all the subjects that Paul treats in this very special epistle is the faith and joy in Christ that filled his heart. Joy in Christ, in fact, is the key thought of the entire epistle, the music that runs through it and the sunshine that radiates over it. The apostle had found the unique joy that comes only to those who have been led by the Holy Spirit to rest their faith and hope in Christ. He was confident that nothing, not even the discouraging circumstances of his captivity, could take that joy away from him.

In this epistle he shares that joy with the Philippians and with Christian readers of every age. As we study this little gem of an epistle, we pray that the Holy Spirit will also fill our hearts with the joy the apostle knew and move us to express and to share that joy with others in what, without Christ, would be a joyless world.

Outline of Philippians

Theme: Sharing Joy

Greeting and Thanksgiving (1:1-11)
I. A Joyful Report From Prison (1:12-26)
   A. Paul's Imprisonment Has Served the Gospel's Cause (1:12-17)

GREETING AND THANKSGIVING
PHILIPPIANS 1:1-11

Greeting

1 Paul and Timothy, servants of Christ Jesus,
To all the saints in Christ Jesus at Philippi, together with the overseers and deacons:

²Grace and peace to you from God our Father and the Lord Jesus Christ.

Paul's letter to the Philippians follows the standard form of letter writing that was used in polite society of the apostle's day. Our letters conclude with the sender's name. In Paul's day the sender mentioned his own name first, then the name of the person or persons addressed. The address was followed by a greeting, then, especially in the apostle's letters, a thanksgiving and prayer. Then came the body of the letter and the conclusion. Included in the conclusions were personal greetings, a farewell, and, in the apostle's letters, a benediction.

Paul, the great missionary apostle, is the inspired author of the epistle to the Philippians. This is one of thirteen New Testament epistles that flowed from his pen. In this epistle Paul associates Timothy with himself, because Timothy seconds what the apostle is saying and fully agrees with the apostle's message. Like Paul, Timothy was well known to the Philippians and deeply interested in their welfare. Timothy had been in Paul's party when the apostle first brought the gospel to the Philippians. He had probably visited the congregation on more than one occasion and was destined to be sent to them again. Paul may even have dictated this epistle to Timothy, as Timothy was with him during much of that first imprisonment in Rome.

"Servants of Christ Jesus" is how Paul describes both Timothy and himself. The term "servant" expresses the apostles' deep devotion to their calling. They were Christ's own possessions, because he had purchased them with his blood and had taken them into his service. Their great aim was to do the Lord's work and to serve him with joy. The Philippians, therefore, should gladly receive the message being sent to them, not because Paul and Timothy were important, but because Jesus is, and in this epistle the apostle is speaking for Jesus.

The recipients of this epistle are "all the saints in Christ Jesus at Philippi." "Saints" is a term regularly used in the New Testament to designate Christians. The word itself means "separated ones." By the Holy Spirit's work in their hearts through the gospel believers have been separated from the world, cleansed from sin and made holy in God's sight. That is the believers' status in Christ Jesus. Saints are sinful human beings to whom God has shown great favor — and to whom he has given great responsibilities. Whenever we meet this term, we ought to be reminded of the dignity God has bestowed on those whom he in love has set apart to be his children, and we ought to be grateful that we are included.

Without trying to distinguish between the true believers and those in the congregation who might be hypocrites, Paul simply addresses all the members of the congregation in Philippi as saints. He extends a special greeting to the "overseers and deacons." Though we do not possess all the details about the structure of the early congregations, it appears that the overseers and deacons were congregational leaders.

Acts 6 indicates that the deacons' responsibilities lay more in the realm of the congregation's physical affairs, while the overseers were probably more concerned with preaching and teaching. Paul's special mention of the overseers and deacons here could well indicate that these leaders had been instrumental in gathering the gift the congregation had sent to him. Good leaders are the Lord's special gifts to Christian congregations. The Philippians had, apparently, been blessed with such leaders.

The apostle greets the Philippians with the familiar words, "grace and peace." These are the key spiritual gifts that believers have in Christ. Grace is God's unmerited favor, the love for the unloveable that moved him to bring about salvation in Christ for a world of sinners. Peace results from grace. It is the spiritual peace that fills believers' hearts through the certainty that their sins have been forgiven and God is at peace with them through Christ. These two words, grace and peace, pronounced on believers as a greeting and a blessing, flood believers' hearts with the joy of salvation and call to mind all that God has done for them in Christ. No more suitable words could be chosen for a greeting to Christians.

Thanksgiving and Prayer

[3] I thank my God every time I remember you. [4] In all my prayers for all of you, I always pray with joy [5] because of your partnership in the gospel from the first day until now, [6] being confident of this, that he who began a good work in you will carry it on to completion until the day of Christ Jesus.

[7] It is right for me to feel this way about all of you, since I have you in my heart; for whether I am in chains or defending and

16

confirming the gospel, all of you share in God's grace with me. [8]God can testify how I long for all of you with the affection of Christ Jesus.

[9]And this is my prayer: that your love may abound more and more in knowledge and depth of insight, [10]so that you may be able to discern what is best and may be pure and blameless until the day of Christ, [11]filled with the fruit of righteousness that comes through Jesus Christ — to the glory and praise of God.

The Apostle Paul enjoyed an excellent relationship with all the congregations he served with the gospel. In all but two of his epistles he followed his greeting with a word of thanks to the Lord for what the gospel had accomplished in the particular congregation to which he was writing. Still, there was something special about the congregation in Philippi, a congregation the apostle himself called "my joy and my crown." Whenever he thought about them and whenever he prayed for the Philippian Christians, a whole host of precious memories flooded into his heart, and each memory filled him with joyful thanksgiving to the Lord.

Whenever he thought about the Philippians and his eventful ministry among them, the apostle must have remembered the special way in which the Lord had called him to bring the gospel to that area of the world: the night vision and the urgent call, "Come over into Macedonia and help us." He must have remembered the first Christian worship service on the European continent, his meeting with a little group of Jewish women who met along the riverbank on the Sabbath day. He must have remembered Lydia, one of that original group of women, who had enthusiastically accepted the gospel, then immediately opened her home as a temporary lodging place for the missionaries and a headquarters for the infant church.

Whenever he remembered the Philippians, Paul must have remembered his imprisonment in Philippi, the miraculous midnight deliverance the Lord had granted to Silas and to him and the subsequent conversion of the jailer and his family. Paul must have remembered how the Philippians had generously sent him a gift to support his gospel work soon after he had left their city, and he must have thought about all the glowing reports he had since received about the Philippians' faith, love and loyalty to the gospel.

In all of these things Paul saw God's gracious hand at work, and for all of them he gave the Lord hearty thanks. Already here in these verses we detect in the apostle's words the positive, joyful note that will continue sounding like heavenly music throughout the entire epistle.

All of these things and more the apostle includes in our text under the phrase "your partnership in the gospel." The Holy Spirit's work in the Philippians' hearts through the gospel had brought them into a wonderful partnership with the apostle and with all other believers. The essence of that partnership — we sometimes also call it "fellowship" — is a mutual sharing in the blessings of forgiveness and salvation won by Christ and in the new spiritual life the Holy Spirit creates in sinners' hearts through faith in Christ.

Believers who have been brought together into a gospel partnership joyfully give expression to their partnership. They do this in many ways. They worship, pray and study God's word together. They joyfully acknowledge one another as brothers and sisters in Christ. They show to one another a special measure of helpfulness and love. They encourage one another in Christian living, and they work together to promote the cause of the gospel in the world.

From the very first day he preached the gospel in Philippi, Paul says, their gospel partnership with the apostle, with one another and with their fellow believers everywhere had been important to the Philippians. They had been wonderfully active in fulfilling their obligations in that partnership, and they had worked diligently to extend it. As more and more believers were added to their congregation, more and more visible evidences of their partnership in the gospel appeared in their individual lives and in their congregational life.

This gospel partnership in which the Philippians shared was a special gift of God's grace to them. Through the gospel God had continued to nourish and strengthen their faith and to fill them with enthusiasm for the Savior's cause. Paul was confident that, through that same gospel, the Lord would continue this gracious work until the day of Christ's return.

The apostle certainly is not advocating overconfidence here. Nor is he implying that once a person has been brought to faith he cannot lose the blessings God has given. In the very next chapter he urges believers to use diligently the spiritual weapons and powers the Lord has given them to fight against sin and temptation and to grow in faith. But here Paul is encouraging believers with God's own promise. God graciously brings believers to faith and assures them that, as they continue to use his word and the sacraments, he will preserve them in faith. Christians' spiritual security, therefore, does not depend on their own sin-tainted efforts. It rests on the promises and the power of God.

His thankful remembrance of the Philippians and their partnership in the gospel, Paul says, was only right, because he had them in his heart. When Paul wrote these words, he was especially conscious of the gospel bond that united him to the Philippians and to all other believers. He was deeply aware of the common grace that they shared. He realized that the cause of the gospel was not just his cause, but the

19

cause of all believers. Paul knew that the outcome of his appeal to the emperor would somehow have an effect on all the believers throughout the Roman empire. He wanted the Philippian Christians to know, therefore, that as he defended and proclaimed the gospel in Rome, he had them and their fellow believers everywhere in his heart.

From the beginning of their lives as Christians to the time of the apostle's imprisonment the Philippians had happily acknowledged the gospel bond that existed between the apostle and themselves. Just lately they had again shown special concern for Paul by sending both a gift and a servant to assist him. Paul knew, too, that the Philippian believers continually remembered him in their prayers. The apostle appreciated all these gestures of Christian concern, and he wanted to assure the Philippians of his deep and personal concern for them.

So he added a personal note to complete the picture of his relationship to the Philippian Christians. Calling on God, the judge of hearts, as his witness, Paul spoke of his earnest longing to be with his Philippian friends again. During his absence from them his heart continued to be filled with the tenderest affection for them, affection founded and patterned on the love of Jesus himself. In that spirit of affection and Christian love Paul wanted to share his joy with the Philippians, if not in person, then certainly by means of this inspired letter, and he wanted the Philippians to read the letter as a genuine outpouring of that same affection and love.

The importance that Paul places on the gospel partnership he shares with the Philippians has much to say also to us. Today we share a gospel partnership with the members of our congregation as well as with the members of our church body, our synod. Our worship life, our mutual support of the Lord's work at home and abroad, our encouragements to each other to live as Christians are all expressions of that partnership. So is the special affection and concern we ought to feel and show for one another.

Our gospel partnership is higher and nobler than ordinary earthly relationships, but too often we tend to regard the precious gospel partnerships of our congregational and synodical memberships too lightly. We are inclined to look on these partnerships, not as precious blessings, but as tiresome burdens and obligations. Only rarely do we regard the individuals with whom we share this partnership as special. Our relationships with all our fellow believers, our attitude toward our synod and its work and the enthusiasm and the zeal with which we go about the tasks the Lord has assigned to us could be significantly improved. We need to see those relationships as the apostle Paul saw them, as elements of our blessed partnership in the gospel. That, in turn, would make our whole spiritual lives more positive and more joyful.

The apostle's prayer of thanksgiving for the Philippians flows naturally from praise to petition. He requests that their love might abound more and more in knowledge and depth of insight. The Philippians have already given ample evidences of their faith and love. Paul's prayer here is that they might grow in faith, as well as in their desire and ability to bring forth the fruits of faith in words and deeds of love. Since believers are still sinners and will never reach perfection here on earth, there is always room for healthy, steady growth in their Christian lives.

Paul prays that their growth in faith and love might be of the proper kind. Unless it flows from a believing knowledge of God's love for sinners in Christ, love is only a vague and unstable human emotion. The person who possesses love

21

without insight or discernment may show great enthusiasm. But if he has no perception, no insight or mature spiritual judgment, his enthusiastic love can easily do more harm than good. Paul's petition here is that the Philippians' love might not stand still or stagnate, but might abound in connection with spiritual knowledge and insight. He prays that their love might overflow its previous limits, ever maturing into a stronger, wiser, nobler, abler love, and that it might be applied in a truly God-pleasing manner in every area of their lives.

As they grow in the mature Christian love that is coupled with knowledge and depth of insight, believers will be able to test what is best. They will be able properly to evaluate the various teachings and philosophies that confront them in their lives and make God-pleasing moral choices. They will grow in their ability to live the Christianity they profess. When the great day of Christ's return comes and the true character of everyone's heart and life is revealed, their lives will be acknowledged by the Lord as lives filled with fruits of faith, and Christ will be truly honored through them.

This beautiful prayer of the apostle for the Philippians is a model for us as we pray for ourselves and for each other. As we make use of the powerful means of grace, we shall experience the joy of growing together in the mature faith that works through insightful love. Then our lives, too, will glorify our Savior, and we shall be found blameless in his sight on the great day of his return.

A JOYFUL REPORT FROM PRISON
PHILIPPIANS 1:12-26

Paul's Imprisonment Has Served the Gospel's Cause

[12]Now I want you to know, brothers, that what has happened to me has really served to advance the gospel. [13]As a result, it has become clear throughout the whole palace guard and to everyone else that I am in chains for Christ. [14]Because of my chains, most of the brothers in the Lord have been encouraged to speak the word of God more courageously and fearlessly.

[15]It is true that some preach Christ out of envy and rivalry, but others out of good will. [16]The latter do so in love, knowing that I am put here for the defense of the gospel. [17]The former preach Christ out of selfish ambition, not sincerely, supposing that they can stir up trouble for me while I am in chains. [18]But what does it matter? The important thing is that in every way, whether from false motives or true, Christ is preached. And because of this I rejoice.

One of the primary reasons that Paul wrote his epistle to the Philippians was to tell them how things were going for him in Rome. The Philippians were concerned about the apostle. They wondered what would happen to him, and they were concerned about the effect his imprisonment would have on the overall cause of the gospel. Would people continue to respond positively to a message whose best known and most eloquent advocate was now a prisoner of the state?

Paul's first words about his situation are intended to lay the Philippians' fears and worries to rest. With enthusiastic joy he reports that the Lord has taken all the negative things

23

that happened to him in connection with his imprisonment and trial and used them to advance the cause of the gospel. Paul's imprisonment and trial have become a tool in God's hands to remove prejudices and obstacles and to provide a positive atmosphere for a clear and effective proclamation of the gospel in the capital city of the world. In his own life the apostle is now experiencing the truth of the divine promise the Lord has earlier given the Roman believers through him: "We know that in all things God works for the good of those who love him, who have been called according to his purpose." That promise remains true for believers of every age, from the greatest apostle to the humblest Christian.

God was working through his imprisonment to advance the cause of the gospel in Rome. That was clear to Paul from at least two important developments. First, Paul's case and consequently the gospel's cause had received favorable publicity, first among the members of the palace guard and then throughout the whole city of Rome. The mention of the palace guard (its official title was the Praetorian guard) would be of particular interest to the Philippian veterans. This well-known military company was a detachment of elite imperial troops stationed in Rome. Its soldiers served, among other things, as the emperor's bodyguard.

Paul doesn't fill in all the details for us here, but apparently members of the guard were also assigned on a rotation basis to guard prisoners like the apostle, who had come to Rome to appeal their cases to Caesar. As Paul awaited his trial, then received his first hearing, he became acquainted with many of the soldiers of the palace guard. These soldiers gradually began to realize that Paul was no ordinary prisoner, and certainly no criminal. As they observed the apostle and heard him speak to his friends, his secretary, his judges and to them, even these hardened soldiers could not help but become interested in Paul's case and the cause for which he stood. It became clear to them that Paul was a prisoner solely for his connection with Jesus Christ, not because he had committed any crime.

The guard members spoke about Paul and his case to one another, to their families and to others in Rome. As a result, the gospel of Christ and the remarkable ambassador who was willing to suffer imprisonment for the sake of the gospel became "front page news," the talk of all Rome. The mistrust and hostility that many in Rome had harbored toward this "new" religion called Christianity were broken down, as the real issue in Paul's case became clear, and the gospel message itself became more generally known. Paul's eloquent defense and confirmation of the gospel at his public hearing likewise served to generate favorable publicity for the gospel throughout the imperial city.

A second positive development was that many of the "brothers in the Lord," that is, believers who were already in Rome before Paul arrived in the city, found new courage to proclaim and confess the gospel. Years earlier a congregation had been founded at Rome. It consisted mostly of Gentile converts. After Paul arrived in the city, large numbers of Jews, including several entire synagogues, were also converted to Christianity. The reaction to Paul's case had produced a positive attitude toward Christianity in Rome, and the Lord was blessing the apostle's testimony of Christ in a marvelous manner. This gave all the believers in Rome fresh courage to identify themselves publicly as Christians and to share the good news of the gospel with others.

One negative note, unfortunately, does creep into this generally positive picture. Those who were now proclaiming the gospel in Rome with such eagerness, the apostle says, did

25

so with two different motives. Some proclaimed Christ out of genuine good will. They truly loved the gospel, and they loved and respected the Lord's apostle. They understood what the Lord was accomplishing through Paul, and they were genuinely encouraged by the apostle's example.

Others, however, proclaimed Christ out of envy and rivalry. It seems that some of the Christians who had been in Rome before Paul arrived in their city became jealous of the apostle's gifts and of all the special attention he received. Hadn't they, after all, been working harder and longer for Christ in Rome? Why should Paul now get all the attention, all the "glory"? Shouldn't they get some, too?

So they continued to take advantage of the favorable atmosphere for proclaiming Christ that the apostle's presence in the city provided, but these Christians did their proclaiming of Christ with a selfish spirit that was interested in their own honor. This envious spirit may not always have been evident, but it was there, and it pained Paul that anyone should preach the gospel out of anything less than pure and loving motives.

Yet Paul was able to keep everything in perspective. He did not excuse those who were preaching from false motives and trying to win applause at his expense, but he did not pity himself, either. Paul realized that the truly important thing was that the gospel was being preached. Some day some would have to answer to God about their false motives, but the Lord was using even those selfish believers, despite their motives to proclaim Christ. Because Christ was being proclaimed and honored, Paul rejoiced.

What a sad thing it is when jealousy and envy spoil the relationship of believers working together for the Lord's cause. "Professional jealousy" can exist between called church workers of differing abilities. Petty jealousies and rivalries may arise among church members, so that they are quick to criticize and work for the Lord and his church on earth in the spirit of envy and strife.

We don't like to admit that such selfish motives creep into the hearts of us all, but we know that is true, so we need to guard our hearts against such a spirit. We need to strive against the desire for personal recognition that so often spoils even our best efforts for our Lord and his church. At the same time let us daily seek from our Lord the pure hearts which will enable us to serve him and his church on earth in the spirit of genuine love and good will. It is comforting, too, to know that the Lord can take even those actions of ours that flow from motives that are less than pure and use them in the service of his kingdom.

Paul Rejoices to Live or Die for Christ

Yes, and I will continue to rejoice, ¹⁹for I know that through your prayers and the help given by the Spirit of Jesus Christ, what has happened to me will turn out for my deliverance. ²⁰I eagerly expect and hope that I will in no way be ashamed, but will have sufficient courage so that now as always Christ will be exalted in my body, whether by life or by death. ²¹For to me, to live is Christ and to die is gain. ²²If I am to go on living in the body, this will mean fruitful labor for me. Yet, what shall I choose? I do not know! ²³I am torn between the two: I desire to depart and be with Christ, which is better by far; ²⁴but it is more necessary for you that I remain in the body. ²⁵Convinced of this, I know that I will remain, and I will continue with all of you for your progress and joy in the faith, ²⁶so that through my being with you again your joy in Christ Jesus will overflow on account of me.

Paul has rejoiced to see his imprisonment advance the cause of the gospel. Now in that same spirit of rejoicing he continues, "What has happened to me will turn out for my deliverance." The English translations have a difficult time trying to catch the real sense of what the apostle is saying here. Dr. Beck probably comes the closest by translating, "(These things . . .) will turn out victoriously for me." From the moment he became a Christian to the time he wrote these words as a prisoner, the Apostle Paul had one great passion: to glorify Christ. As he surveyed the situation in which he now found himself, he was confident that no matter how it would finally turn out for him, whether he lived or died, Christ would be glorified. For Paul that was reason for joy.

Paul's confidence that Christ would be glorified through him was not just an overconfident boast. He based it on the Philippians' prayers for him and the help the Holy Spirit would give. The apostle knew that not only the Philippian congregation, but all of Christendom was praying for him that he might give a good confession before his Roman judges. Prayer for one another is an important part of believers' partnership in the gospel, and Jesus assures believers that such prayers are heard and answered.

Furthermore, Paul was confident that the Holy Spirit would be with him to supply him with all that was necessary for glorifying Christ. Jesus had promised the original disciples that, when they were haled before earthly judges, the Spirit would be with them to put the right words into their mouths. Paul knew that promise of Jesus also held true for him. The Spirit was indeed using Paul and the public testimony he gave at his trial to glorify Christ.

Paul had experienced the Spirit's help at his first hearing. He was sure the Spirit would continue to be with him, to equip him with a courageous faith and the right words so that he would fearlessly continue to confess Christ before his judges and before all of Rome. Christ would be glorified as a result of his testimony, so Paul could say that his imprisonment and trial and everything connected with it would turn out victoriously for him — even if he would be condemned and put to death.

The first phase of Paul's trial appears to have gone well. Every indication pointed to a favorable outcome, but he realized that the verdict could still go against him and could even result in his execution. But even that grim prospect could not diminish the apostle's joy, for he knew that the Spirit would use either his life or his death to glorify Christ.

If Paul lived, if he was acquitted and released, he would continue his apostolic labors and do and suffer even more for Christ. If he died, he would go to the Lord with an unshaken faith and a song in his heart. He would give the ultimate testimony of martyrdom as evidence of his commitment to the cause of Christ. Either way, it would be evident to everyone what the Lord, by his grace, can accomplish in his children.

The apostle's great desire to glorify Christ in living and dying is beautifully summarized in the familiar words of verse 21. These words have been described as Paul's "magnificent obsession." "For to me, to live is Christ and to die is gain." From the dramatic moment on the Damascus road when he came to know the risen and glorified Christ to his anxious days as a prisoner for Christ in the world capital, all of Paul's life and living were Christ.

By grace he had been made a new creature in Christ. In baptism he had put on Christ. Daily he lived in the knowledge that his sins were covered with Christ's righteousness. He drew his strength for living from Christ. His constant desire was to know Christ more deeply and to serve him more completely. Paul regarded himself as a slave of Christ with no will of his own, totally submissive to his master's will. Christ was the secret, the source, the summary of the apostle's life. Christ filled his life with joy and enabled him effectively to communicate that joy to others.

If a believer's life is Christ, then it naturally follows that "to die is gain." Throughout their earthly lives believers are united with Christ by faith, but their oneness with Christ, their knowledge of him and service to him are imperfect, blurred and clouded by sin. At the moment of their physical death all that will change for the better. What believers possess spiritually by faith here on earth they will have by sight in eternity. In eternal life they will see Christ face to face and glorify him with perfect service, adoration and joy. As Paul saw it, death was gain, for death would bring more of him to Christ and more of Christ to him. If Christ was being glorified in the apostle's life on earth, how much more would Christ be glorified through Paul's perfect worship and service in eternity.

Having set forth the great principles that govern a Christian's living and dying in Christ, Paul applied those principles directly to his own situation. He knew that a favorable verdict at his trial would mean more fruitful work for him. Being set free would permit him to take up his apostolic labors again. He would again be able to preach the gospel openly, among old friends and in new places. That kind of work is always fruitful labor. Jesus himself guarantees it. Through such fruitful labor, of course, Christ would be glorified.

Yet, Paul says, if the choice between living and dying were left strictly up to him, he would have a hard time making a decision. Like every believer who truly knows and loves the Savior, Paul had an intense desire to depart from this life and to be with Christ. He longed to be free from the suffering, trouble and pain that characterize life in this sinful world and enter into the perfect joy of heaven. There was no doubt in the apostle's mind that at the very moment his soul departed this life it would be with the Lord.

Eternal life with Christ, Paul says, is better than life here on earth. Despite the obvious advantages death would bring to him, however, Paul also felt hard pressed by another consideration. "It is more necessary for you," he tells the Philippians, "that I remain in the body." The apostle was aware of the fact that the Philippians, as well as many of the other recently converted Christians, still needed him.

The Philippian congregation was less than ten years old. Many of its members had only recently turned from idolatry. The congregation had its weaknesses and was surrounded by dangers. If it was now suddenly deprived of its beloved apostle and his strong leadership and guidance, the congregation's development could be seriously hindered. Personal advantage for the apostle lay with departing from this life to be with Christ, but "necessity," or advantage for his readers lay with his continuing to live on.

Paul recognized that the choice of whether he lived or died was not up to him. The Lord would make that choice for him. But on the basis of the factors he had just mentioned the apostle permitted himself what we might call an "inspired speculation." Because he was convinced that longer life for him would mean fruit resulting from more apostolic labors, and because he knew that such labors were still needed by the young churches, he was confident that he would be allowed to continue his work on earth, at least for a little while longer.

If it was God's plan for him to forego for a time the glories of heaven so that he could continue to live and labor for the gospel, Paul would not only accept it, he would rejoice in it, because Christ would continue to be glorified through his apostolic work. What special joy the Philippians and the apostle would share after the dark days of his imprisonment if they could be reunited to rejoice in their partnership in the gospel and to praise the Lord for his mercy in reuniting them.

All the historical evidence we possess indicates that the apostle's expectations were fulfilled. Apparently he was set free from this particular imprisonment and allowed by the Lord to carry on his apostolic labors, at least for a few more years. It is also quite likely that Paul did see the Philippians again before he was arrested and imprisoned for the second and final time. That second imprisonment and its outcome are discussed in Paul's last letter, 2 Timothy.

Paul's eloquent and joy-filled words in this section express the attitude every Christian ought to take toward both living and dying. For a Christian, life is Christ. Real living is impossible apart from Christ. The great goal of every Christian's life ought to be to serve and glorify Christ. If Christ is truly our life, our obsession with him and our joy in him will be evident in everything we do. Our thinking and planning will all be centered in him, and our words and actions will constantly testify of our commitment to him who has made us new spiritual creatures through faith in him.

Living such a life and reflecting such a commitment is not always easy. There are many hindrances and enemies, including the sinful nature within us that wants us to live only for ourselves. Like Paul, though, we can find the strength to live for Christ in what the Holy Spirit supplies us through the means of grace. We can confidently pray for the Spirit's rich supply. As we grow daily in grace and knowledge and living faith, we can make the words of Paul's confession our own: "For to me, to live is Christ." In such living alone we can find real satisfaction and joy.

We can also learn much from a consideration of the apostle's attitude toward death. The apostle did not go all to pieces at the prospect of death. He was not so attached to this life that he regarded death as an unwelcome intruder. For the apostle death was gain, a personal advantage, because he knew it would mean a passing from a troublesome life marred by sin to a perfect existence with the Savior. Paul was ready to go and be with the Savior at any time. Yet, if it was the Savior's will for him to live and work on, he would gladly do that, until the Savior called him.

The apostle's view of death avoids two extremes: an undue attachment to this impermanent life and an impatient desire for death. The former is a danger for Christians at any age. The latter can be a danger especially to suffering or aged Christians. A suffering Christian may humbly beseech the Lord to deliver him from his troubles, but not every wish to die is a pious wish. If it flows simply from a desire to escape the obligations of life or to be relieved of its burdens, it is only selfishness. Sometimes a whining desire to die is nothing less than a impatient complaint against God. In the apostle's words, though, we note no impatience, no complaint, only a joyful willingness to glorify Christ in life or death, as the time and circumstances please him. This is an attitude worthy of imitation by every Christian.

ENCOURAGEMENTS TO LIVE LIVES
OF GOSPEL JOY
PHILIPPIANS 1:27-4:9

Stand Firm in the Gospel

[27]Whatever happens, conduct yourselves in a manner worthy of the gospel of Christ. Then, whether I come and see you or only hear about you in my absence, I will know that you stand firm in one spirit, contending as one man for the faith of the gospel [28]without being frightened in any way by those who oppose you. This is a sign to them that they will be destroyed, but that you will be saved — and that by God. [29]For it has been granted to you on behalf of Christ not only to believe on him, but also to suffer for him, [30]since you are going through the same struggle you saw I had, and now hear that I still have.

With these verses the apostle closes his report to the Philippians about himself, and he begins a series of instructions, or encouragements which continue throughout most of the rest of the epistle. Whatever happens to him personally, Paul tells the Philippians, whether he comes to them as he expects, or remains absent from them, they should conduct themselves in a manner worthy of the gospel. The root meaning of the verb Paul uses here is "exercise citizenship." The Philippians, many of them Roman army veterans and their families, were especially proud of their Roman citizenship. The apostle wanted to remind them that as Christians they possessed a citizenship even more important than the earthly citizenship of which they were so proud. The Philippian believers were citizens of Jesus' spiritual kingdom. As their conduct in so many ways gave evidence of their cherished Roman citizenship, it should, in even more ways, reflect their spiritual citizenship.

To exercise citizenship in a manner worthy of the gospel means to live in a manner which will truly give evidence of the new spiritual life the gospel has produced in one's heart. When the gospel enters human hearts and joins sinful human beings to Christ by faith, it changes people's lives. It moves and empowers human beings, who previously lived only for themselves, to live in love to God and to their fellow men. Paul urges the Philippians here to show what the gospel has done for them and in them by living lives that will bring honor to God and glorify the Lord whom the gospel proclaims.

If they exercise their spiritual citizenship in accord with what the gospel has done in and for them, the Philippians will "stand firm in one spirit, contending as one man for the faith of the gospel, without being frightened in any way by those who oppose you." Believers who exercise citizenship worthy of the gospel will take a firm stand on the gospel. They will hold fast to the gospel teachings they have received and will not compromise with error. They will live in harmony with one another, struggling side by side to defend and promote the gospel in a hostile world.

Nor will they fear the enemies that oppose them. Because of their Christian confession the Philippian believers faced many enemies. (Paul will further describe those enemies in chapter 3.) But believers who stand firm in the gospel need not be frightened by any of their enemies, no matter how fierce or how powerful they may appear. Rather, they can confidently and courageously carry out their struggle against those enemies, knowing that the Lord is on their side.

The very fact that God gives believers fearlessness in the face of their enemies is a sign of the enemies' destruction and believers' salvation. When their enemies see the fearless courage with which the little band of believers stands up for Jesus and the gospel, they will have to concede that believers have working for them a power far greater than any human power, a power that they simply cannot overcome.

Finally, the apostle personally identifies with the Philippians by reminding them that as they struggle on behalf of the gospel, they stand on common ground with him. Many of the Philippians had personally witnessed some of the conflicts the apostle endured. They remembered when he first brought the gospel to their city and how he had been slandered, mobbed, flogged and thrown into a Roman dungeon. They also remembered how the apostle had remained steadfast and how from the depths of the prison he and his missionary partner Silas sang hymns of praise to the Lord.

In this letter the Philippians could read again about the apostle's bonds and about how those who were encouraged by Satan were raising up affliction for him. The apostle's entire career as a Christian and as a missionary had been a constant struggle, requiring great exertion against powerful foes. Yet in this conflict the apostle received daily strength from the Lord. As he battled on, he could still daily rejoice.

As they faced their enemies, the Philippians were engaged in the same struggle. The archenemy was the same. The cause was the same, and the source of strength for the struggle was also the same. The joy in the Lord Jesus that they could experience in their struggle was the same, and the ultimate victory was the same. Just knowing this should encourage the Philippians in their daily struggles and fill their hearts with fresh courage and joy.

Our constant aim as Christians, too, is to exercise our citizenship in a manner worthy of the gospel, to reflect in our lives the gracious work that the Holy Spirit, through the gospel, has accomplished in us. If that is truly our aim, and if we daily, consciously seek the Spirit's help to accomplish it, our lives, too, will be characterized by firm loyalty to the gospel, by harmony with one another, and by fearlessness in the face of powerful enemies. Like the first-century Philippians, twentieth-century believers have many enemies to fight, people and forces and philosophies from atheism to Zen. Their ultimate instigator is Satan, and their common aim is to silence the gospel and blunt its impact in the world.

As we fight the battle, we can constantly be encouraged by the realization that we are fighting the very same battle that faithful believers like the Apostle Paul and the Philippians have fought, and we can rejoice in the promise that the Lord will also provide to us the spiritual gifts we need to overcome our enemies and win the ultimate victory: steadfastness, harmony and fearlessness, all of which signify our enemies' ultimate defeat and our final victory.

Live in Harmony and Humility with One Another

2 If you have any encouragement from being united with Christ, if any comfort from his love, if any fellowship with the Spirit, if any tenderness and compassion, ²then make my joy complete by being like-minded, having the same love, being one in spirit and purpose. ³Do nothing out of selfish ambition or vain conceit, but in humility consider others better than ourselves. ⁴Each of you should look not only to your own interests, but also to the interests of others.

If the Philippians and other believers are to stand firm against the enemies of the gospel that threaten them from without, they must first be firmly united among themselves.

Paul has already spoken of "standing firm in one spirit." Now he expands on that thought, turning his encouragement inward to the matter of believers' relationships with one another. The apostle's appeal here is thoroughly evangelical, or gospel-based. He speaks to the Philippians' hearts, reminding them of the gospel blessings that are theirs in Christ, then appealing to them on the basis of those blessings. With four short, powerful conditional clauses Paul reminds the Philippians that they have indeed been encouraged by Christ, comforted by his love, made spiritually new and alive by the Spirit's work in their hearts and blessed by the Spirit with the gifts of tenderness and compassion. So he has a right to assume that all he is about to request of the Philippians will naturally follow.

The Philippians had already brought much joy to the apostle. Their partnership in the gospel, their faith and love, their generosity all brought him joy every time he thought about them or prayed for them. But there was one more thing the Philippians could strive to do, Paul says, that would truly make his joy complete. That one thing was to seek a greater measure of harmony in their dealings and relationships with one another.

These words of the apostle have led some Bible students to conclude that pride and internal strife were problems for the Philippian congregation. Perhaps they were. Later on, in chapter 4, the apostle mentions a specific personal rivalry between two of the congregation's prominent women. But whether more such problems existed in the congregation or not, the apostle felt that the Phlippians needed encouragement in this particular area of their Christian lives.

And what congregation doesn't? Where sinners are living and working together with sinners, pride and selfishness are always rearing their ugly heads. The devil works particularly hard to use those products of each member's sinful nature to disrupt the congregation's work through disharmony and strife. In flourishing congregations, where many members are knowledgeable and gifted, there is always the danger of the more gifted members looking down on the less gifted, and of the less gifted envying the more gifted. And it is always characteristic of human nature to minimize one's own weaknesses and to exaggerate one's own strengths, while doing just the opposite when observing the weaknesses and strengths of others. These things can severely retard the spiritual growth of any congregation.

The Apostle Paul regarded the selfishness and pride which disrupt congregational harmony as particularly troublesome and dangerous sins. This is evident from the fact that he issues warnings against them in just about every one of his epistles. Other examples of such warnings are found in Galatians 5:25,26, 1 Corinthians 1:10-17, Ephesians 4:2,3. So, whether lack of harmony was more of a problem in the Philippian congregation than in others or not, the Philippian believers certainly needed the Christ-centered encouragements of our text. And so do we.

Paul encourages the Philippians to strive for greater unity of disposition, lowliness and helpfulness. *Unity of disposition* is the common view of life that believers ought to share, because they have been united by the Spirit in a common faith in the Lord Jesus. "Our fears, our hopes, our aims are one," a hymnwriter puts it, "our comforts and our cares." Believers who are "like-minded" judge all things by the word of God. They love one another with the unselfish kind of love that gives without expecting anything in return and finds its motive and example in the love of Christ. And like-minded Christians agree on the great common goal of promoting Jesus' kingdom in the world. Though they may be different in many other respects, believers think alike spiritually. And they ought to be working and praying continually for a greater unity of disposition.

Lowliness, or humble-mindedness, is also a key New Testament concept, a distinctive mark of the committed Christian. Lowliness is the opposite of the selfishness and pride of our corrupt and sinful natures. First century society placed little value on lowliness. It regarded it, in fact, as the equivalent of cowardice and equated pride and self-assertiveness with manhood. The non-Christian world today thinks in the same way. Books and classes offering assertiveness training and ever more effective methods of exercising power and "looking out for number one" are tremendously popular and profitable. But the attitude of a heart changed by God's grace is no longer "me first and everybody else after me, if at all." Rather it is an attitude that humbly and lovingly places the interests of others before one's own.

When he urges believers to "consider others better than themselves," Paul is not advocating a false modesty. He does not want talented believers to deny their special gifts or hide or neglect them. He is laying down a general principle that should govern believers' relationships with each other. A humble child of God, no matter how many or how few his gifts may be, will strive to put the best construction on everything the neighbor does. He will happily acknowledge and respect whatever gifts the neighbor has, be they many or few. In everything the humble Christian will strive to give the neighbor first consideration.

When each one in a community of Christians considers the others better than himself in this way, a marvelous harmony has to result. No one in that community is looked down upon, but everyone is looked up to, as all willingly give of themselves to show kindness to others. Paul himself had learned the grace of lowliness well.

Can the same be said of us? Or does our self-assertiveness show that our lives are not as Spirit-directed as they should be? It is difficult for Christians to put their faith into practice when it means adopting attitudes and actions that are radically different from those of the society in which they live. But right here is where true Christians show their colors and sham Christians are exposed. Only the gospel can give us, who are at the same time both saints and sinners, the spiritual strength we need to live the lives of lowliness that will clearly distinguish us as genuine followers of our lowly Lord.

Harmony becomes practical among Christians in *helpfulness*, when each believer strives to do those things that serve and help the neighbor in every possible way. The world's way is to look out for oneself. It considers the needs of others only when it sees some ultimate advantage for itself, but believers' concern for their neighbors' interest will supersede concern for their own. And again, what a sure means that will be of promoting God-pleasing harmony among Christians.

⁵Your attitude should be the same as that of Christ Jesus:
    ⁶Who, being in very nature God,
       did not consider equality with God
          something to be grasped,
    ⁷but made himself nothing,
       taking the very nature of a servant,
       being made in human likeness.
    ⁸And being found in appearance as a man,
       he humbled himself
       and became obedient to death —
          even death on a cross!

41

⁹**Therefore God exalted him to the highest place**
  and gave him the name that is above every name,
¹⁰**that at the name of Jesus every knee should bow,**
  in heaven and on earth and under the earth,
¹¹**and every tongue confess that Jesus Christ is Lord,**
  to the glory of the God the Father.

The inclination of our sinful human nature is not to humility, love and service, but to selfishness, so triumph over self is the great necessity for believers who truly desire to put their Christian faith into practice. In the familiar words of this section the apostle underscores his previous encouragement to the Philippians. He points them and all believers to the Lord Jesus as both the perfect example and the ultimate source of strength for living lives of Christian humilty and love.

The attitude which accompanies triumph over self and results in true harmony among Christians is found perfectly in Christ. The more thoroughly believers come to know Christ, the more completely Christ and his love will fill their hearts. The more they are in Christ and Christ is in them, the more Christ-like and unselfish they will be in their attitudes and actions. So, by way of encouragement to Christians to adopt their Savior's attitude as their own, Paul offers this magnificent description of the attitude of Christ.

The apostle's words are offered here as encouragement, but they are much more than that. Suddenly, perhaps surprisingly, they expand into a significant doctrinal statement, one of the great New Testament summaries of the humiliation and exaltation of our Savior. With a loftiness and dignity of style which well suit the profound nature of his subject matter, the apostle takes us by the hand and leads us to see the divine mysteries of the person of Christ and the work which brought about our salvation.

The apostle begins this significant section of his epistle with an unparalleled description of the humiliation of the God-man. In order to understand Jesus' humiliation, we must first understand that he is God "in very nature," as Paul says. From all eternity Jesus has been one with the Father, truly God. His eternal existence as God is unshakeable and unchangeable. Jesus' divine nature is not capable of experiencing humiliation, but Jesus, while fully retaining his divine nature, took on a true human nature. He was conceived by the Holy Ghost and born of the Virgin Mary. He who is true God from all eternity became a true man and dwelt among men. This we call the incarnation, and we accept it as one of the great mysteries of the Christian faith.

In Jesus' incarnation the human nature Jesus assumed shared in all the characteristics of his divine nature. The two natures are now perfectly united. After the incarnation the Bible speaks of one divine-human Christ, the God-man. Jesus possesses all the fulness of the divinity. Yet, because he is truly man as well as truly God, he could and did humble himself for us. Because our human understanding of divine things is limited by sin, we cannot fully fathom this, but God clearly reveals these awe-inspiring truths to us in his word. We humbly accept them in grateful faith.

Jesus is indeed true God, equal with the Father in power, authority and majesty, and he possesses all the characteristics of God. This he clearly demonstrated during his earthly ministry. Here was a man who could read the hearts of men, feed multitudes, control the weather, cast out devils, heal the sick and even raise the dead. Those who observed him at closest range had to declare, "You are the Christ, the Son of the living God." Jesus was and is in very nature God.

Nevertheless, the apostle tells us, he "did not consider equality with God something to be grasped." Jesus was well

43

aware of the fact that he is God. He knew perfectly that from all eternity he possessed all the majesty of God and that he possessed it fully also during the days of his earthly ministry. But Jesus did not consider this something to be exhibited or displayed for his personal self-advancement and glory.

In Paul's day victorious generals and other public figures would frequently honor themselves and their achievements by using their "moment in the sun" to erect monuments to themselves and their achievements. Today, too, the great men of the world frequently use the privileges and trappings of their offices to enhance their reputations, further their careers, perhaps even line their pockets.

Jesus, though he was God in very nature, did not appear on earth to glorify himself. He did not look for his own advantage. Nor did he arbitrarily use the divine privileges and powers he possessed to satisfy passing fancies or to gain earthly fame and power. If those had been the reasons for which he assumed his human nature, it would have been useless for him to assume it. The mission he received from the Father simply could not be combined with a gaudy display of divine majesty. So there was no such display. When he who is in very nature God came to this earth, he considered the mission and the work for which he had assumed his human nature. He considered us, and he humbled himself.

In accomplishing his humiliation, the God-man "made himself nothing, taking the very nature of a servant, being made in human likeness." Human language struggles to give adequate expression to the greatness of what Jesus did. The expression "made himself nothing" literally means "emptied himself." Jesus, of course, did not empty himself of the deity, as some wrongly teach. He was and ever remained true God. At times, even in his state of humiliation, he clearly gave evidence of the divine characteristics and powers he still possessed. We think for example, of the miracles, his transfiguration, or even the sudden display of his almighty power that he showed his enemies in the Garden of Gethsemane.

The divine nature was always there, and all that his deity bestowed on his human nature was always his as the God-man. But during his earthly life and ministry Jesus emptied himself of the *full and constant use* of all the prerogatives of his divinity. He laid aside the unlimited exercise of his power and did not always use or demand his rights as God. Instead, he "took on the nature of a servant." It was as if he covered the glory of his divine majesty with the tattered rags of a beggar. He became altogether lowly. He became like every other human being — lowlier, in fact, than most — in his earthly manner of living. Though he himself was sinless, he assumed human nature in the weakened condition in which we have it, burdened with the consequences of sin. Although he is the Lord of the universe, he was born in a stable. He never possessed earthly property or wealth. He was despised by many of his contemporaries. He placed himself under the demands of God's law. He took on the nature of a servant while he retained, but did not always use, the full power and majesty of God.

Jesus' emptying himself of the full and constant use of his divine majesty and taking on a servant's form was a necessary part of his office as our Redeemer. If he had lived on earth only as the disciples saw him on the Mount of Transfiguration, his redemptive obedience to the law as our substitute, as well as his rejection, suffering and death would never have taken place, and our salvation never would have been won.

What a remarkable difference there is between the way earthly rulers or conquerors seek victories and the way Jesus

Let Him Be Crucified

gained the greatest victory of all for us. Earthly rulers seek victories through strength. They are forever building up weaponry, armies and alliances to guarantee power for themselves. Jesus worked to gain his victory for us in the very opposite way. He divested himself of the full use of his power and became altogether lowly in order to become the substitute for the sinful world and carry out the Father's plan to save sinful mankind.

With particular reverence St. Paul describes for us the lowest depths to which the humiliation of the God-man took him. This humiliation began at the moment the only-begotten Son of God took on a human nature and entered our world. It did not end until he died on the cross. Not only did Jesus humble himself to become man among men. Not only did he live an earthly existence that was altogether humble and lowly. For man's sake he lowered himself to depths to which no other man has ever gone or could ever go when he "became obedient to death . . . on a cross."

That someone dies on a cross is not an altogether unknown experience among human beings, but Jesus' death on the cross went beyond ordinary human experience, because it was no ordinary death. Death on a cross was a shameful death, the most shameful death a man could die. It was a form of death reserved for the vilest criminals and slaves. It was an excruciatingly painful death. Even more significantly, it was a kind of death cursed by God.

In Old Testament Israel, after a wrongdoer had been put to death, the civil laws prescribed that his dead body be nailed to a post or a tree. This was to impress on the people that that individual, by his transgression, had suffered the ultimate curse of being cut off from God and his believing people. If, in the sight of God, the hanging of a *dead body* signified his curse, how much more would the hanging of a

47

living person be considered a curse, especially when that person was experiencing anguish beyond description. How deliberately and heavily the words fall as the apostle describes the ultimate humiliation of the God-man: EVEN DEATH ON A CROSS.

The shame and degradation of this slave's death made many, like Paul himself before his conversion, absolutely sure that Jesus could not be the Messiah. The lowliness simply did not conform to what they expected the Messiah to be. So the cross of Jesus became a "stumbling block" (1 Corinthians 1:23) to many, especially among the Jews, and still remains "a stone that causes men to stumble and a rock that makes them fall."

But Holy Scripture's clear answer to all human protests is that Jesus' humiliation was in fulfillment of the Scriptures. It was a voluntary act by which Jesus, as the substitute for the entire human race, bore our sins and took our curse to carry out the Father's plan for our salvation. The depth of Jesus' humiliation was at the same time the height of his self-giving, self-sacrificing love. He in whom the Godhead dwelt in bodily form hung on a post of wood as one accursed. He was charged by God with the collective sin and guilt of the world and was forsaken by God into the torments of hell. This is the noblest act of love the world has ever seen, the mystery of the gospel into which the angels desire to look.

And it was all done to benefit us. Because Jesus took our sins, God declares us sinless in his sight. Because Jesus paid for our guilt, we are set free. In God's marvelous great exchange our sins were charged to Christ and his righteousness credited to us. By his humiliation Jesus reconciled us to the God from whom our sins had separated us.

Now, Paul says, we as Jesus' followers are to imitate his lowly-mindedness and self-sacrificing love. If we truly understand the significance of what the God-man did for us, can we refuse to heed this admonition? Can we live selfishly when we belong to such an unselfish Lord? Can we refuse to relinquish our rights or to suffer wrong at the hands of others when love requires it? He became obedient to death for us, and by faith we now have the mind of Christ. Shall we not willingly serve one another for his sake? Shall we not joyfully make those relatively small sacrifices by which we serve one another and thus give evidence that we truly have the mind of Christ?

But the mighty basis on which Paul's admonition rests includes not only Christ's humiliation. It also includes his exaltation. As the God-man, Christ willingly humbled himself for us and for our salvation, but this humiliation was not a permanent thing. It was only for a definite, limited time, and it was undertaken only to accomplish a specific purpose. When that purpose was successfully achieved and man's salvation was fully accomplished, Jesus' humiliation ceased forever.

When Jesus' mission was completed "God exalted him to the highest place." God himself thereby crowned the work that Jesus had done and declared it perfect and complete. In his *state of humiliation* Jesus, the God-man, laid aside the full and complete use of his divine powers, covering them with the "beggar's cloak" of lowly obedience. In his state of *exaltation* the beggar's cloak, the slave's form, has been dropped, and Jesus no longer treats with restraint the fact that he is God.

Yes, Jesus is still the God-man, but he is no longer subject to the weakness and the frailty of fallen humanity. No longer does he use his divine qualities and powers in only a limited or restricted way. Now he fully exercises his majesty as the exalted God-man to rule over everything in heaven and on earth. The God-man, who once humbled himself to the lowest depths to save our race, is now exalted to the loftiest heights as the King of kings and Lord of lords.

The Apostles' Creed lists the various events of Jesus' exaltation: "He descended into hell; the third day he rose again from the dead; he ascended into heaven and sitteth on the right hand of God the Father Almighty; from thence he shall come to judge the quick and the dead." What a glorious victory these words describe. Jesus, our Savior, having successfully completed his redemptive work for us, openly triumphed over the forces of hell. Death had to relinquish its hold on him. Earth could no longer contain him. Heaven opened its doors to receive him. Jesus, our victorious Savior, now holds in his hands the reins of the universe. He rules all things in heaven and on earth in the interest of his believers, and he will come again to end this age, judge the world, and take his believers to be with him and to share his glory in eternal life.

By virtue of his exaltation, Jesus has received "the name that is above every name." He who in his humiliation made himself nothing has in his exaltation a name and a reputation second to none. His name, spoken with contempt by his enemies, especially by those who condemned him to death as a blasphemer, is the only "name under heaven given to men by which we must be saved." Only through Jesus' name, and through faith in his name and the gospel revelation which stands behind it, can sinners be saved. On their relationship to Jesus and his name depend the eternal destinies of all human beings. Either they accept Jesus and his saving revelation of himself by faith and are saved, or they reject him and are lost. We who have been called to faith by the Spirit through the gospel rejoice in the privilege of knowing and confessing that name above all others, the name of Jesus, our exalted prophet, priest and king.

In his humiliation Jesus submitted to the reproach and rejection of sinful men. In his exaltation it is the Father's will that he receive the homage of all created beings. "At the name of Jesus," Paul concludes this grand paragraph, "every knee should bow, in heaven and on earth and under the earth, and every tongue confess that Jesus Christ is Lord, to the glory of God the Father." All created beings must and will confess Jesus as Lord: the saints and angels in heaven, all human beings on earth, even the demons and the damned in hell.

The only question is how and with what spirit they will make that confession. Even now heaven rings with the perfect praise of the saints and angels. On earth sinful and imperfect believers faintly echo that heavenly praise. On judgment day the whole universe will stand before Jesus, the exalted judge. His glory and majesty will be fully revealed to all. Every knee will bow and every tongue will confess Jesus as Lord. Unbelievers, of course, will make that confession to their shame and disgrace. The devils will openly admit their eternal frustration. But believers on earth and in heaven will rejoice on that great day to confess together the most important truth in all the universe. They will joyfully confess throughout eternity that Jesus Christ is Lord. This universal acknowledgement will also glorify the Father, who sent Jesus into the world on his saving mission and exalted him as a consequence of that mission's success.

The humiliation and exaltation of Jesus were unique, because his person is unique. By his humiliation Jesus, the God-man, satisfied divine justice, atoned for the world's sin and earned perfect righteousness for sinners, and he alone merited the super-exaltation that confirmed the success of his work.

In that unique and redemptive sense none of us can be like Jesus, but the apostle urges us Christians in our renewed lives to imitate the spirit of lowliness and humility that was basic to all of Jesus' acts of self-renunciation for us. Such a spirit is also what Jesus seeks when he says, "If anyone would come after me, he must deny himself and take up his cross and follow me." Believers who cultivate this attitude and follow in Christ's steps of humility have the promise that they will also share in the exalted Savior's glory. "If we died with him," Paul tells Timothy, "we will also live with him; if we endure, we will also reign with him."

Christians do not earn a share of Christ's glory by their lowliness and suffering for Jesus' sake. The glory is theirs as a free gift. Nevertheless, to encourage believers in lives of lowliness lived for him and to his glory, the Lord graciously promises that in eternity he will acknowledge lives of self-sacrificing service as evidences that believers were truly loyal to him. And, even though they do not deserve any reward, he will reward believers for lowly, humble service. We call that the "reward of grace." The Christian's life, like Jesus' life, travels the path from humility to glory, from cross to crown, because Jesus has graciously determined that it should be that way.

Moved by the perfect example of our Savior, therefore, and empowered by his Spirit's work in our hearts through the gospel, let us strive to cultivate Christ's attitude of self-sacrificing humility, that we may follow him through life's humiliation to heaven's glory. Let us joyfully and confidently confess him as our Lord and invite others also to confess him. When he at last reveals himself as judge of all the world, he will acknowledge us as his own, and we will join the saints and angels in singing unending hymns of praise to him and the Father in the eternal glory before his shining throne.

Live Blameless Lives in a Godless World

¹²Therefore, my dear friends, as you have always obeyed — not only in my presence, but now much more in my absence — continue to work out your salvation with fear and trembling, ¹³for it is God who works in you to will and to act according to his good purpose.

¹⁴Do everything without complaining or arguing, ¹⁵so that you may become blameless and pure, children of God without fault in a crooked and depraved generation, in which you shine like stars in the universe ¹⁶as you hold out the word of life — in order that I may boast on the day of Christ that I did not run or labor for nothing. ¹⁷But even if I am being poured out like a drink offering on the sacrifice and service coming from your faith, I am glad and rejoice with all of you. ¹⁸So you too should be glad and rejoice with me.

Although he has digressed a bit to treat in detail the subject of Christ's humiliation and exaltation, the apostle is still offering Christians encouragement to "conduct yourselves in a manner worthy of the gospel." In these verses he shows believers how living their lives as Christians will both set them apart in an unbelieving society and bring benefit to that society. The apostle's encouragement here is quite similar to that which Jesus gives in the Sermon on the Mount, when he reminds his disciples that they are the salt of the earth and the light of the world and encourages them to let their light shine.

Paul's words show genuine Christian tact. He calls the Philippians his dear friends, thus placing into his encouragement the appeal of personal love. He praises them for their past obedience. In the New Testament, especially in Paul's writings, the term "obedience" is sometimes used as a synonym for faith. Here it no doubt includes both faith and living the kind of lives that result from faith, that "conduct worthy of the gospel." Since they had become Christians, and especially when the apostle had been personally present with them, the Philippians had shown real obedience to the gospel. They had eagerly accepted the apostle's instruction and put it into practice in their lives. Now, in a very positive way Paul urges them to continue to live in that same way and to do so even more in his absence.

Sometimes Christians tend to relax a little spiritually when a respected spiritual leader is absent. Ask the average parish pastor what happens to church attendance when the members of his congregation know he is going to be away on vacation. Paul does not want the Philippians to let down or relax spiritually when he is away from them. Rather, he wants them to be even more spiritually alert, even more deeply concerned about their souls' welfare in his absence than they were when he was present. They are to continually expend the spiritual effort to "work out your salvation with fear and trembling."

These words of the apostle might at first seem to have a strange ring to them. They might even lead us to wonder if Christians, after all, have to work to earn their own salvation. But that cannot be true. If it were, Paul would be contradicting everything Scripture consistently teaches about the free salvation of sinners by God's grace. Scripture clearly teaches that salvation is a gift. Sinners receive it by faith in Jesus, and that faith is also a gift. Mankind's salvation is perfect and complete in Christ.

But if the apostle is not saying that salvation is something that human beings can earn, what is he saying here? Paul uses the word "salvation" here in a broad sense. He refers not only to believers' coming to faith and receiving the gift of eternal life, but also to their continuing in faith until they enter into eternal life. Generally, believers must continue to live in this sinful world while they await the completed salvation of eternity. It is to such waiting believers, who are still coping with all the challenges and temptations of life in the world, that Paul directs the encouragement, "Continue to work out your salvation with fear and trembling."

Before they are brought to faith, human beings are totally incapable of any positive spiritual working. "As for you," Paul tells the Ephesian believers, "you were dead in your transgressions and sins," (Ephesians 2:1). But then he goes on, "But because of his great love for us, God, who is rich in mercy, made us alive with Christ" (2:4). When God saves sinners by bringing them to faith in Jesus through the gospel, he makes them spiritually alive in Christ. Believers are now capable of spiritual working and the spiritual effort Paul calls for in our text. This is not a working which earns, or tries to earn salvation. It is a working by which believers, who know that they have been saved by the blood of Christ, make the best use of the spiritual gifts and powers with which the Holy Spirit has supplied them to grow in faith, bring forth the fruits of faith, and remain steadfast in faith unto eternal life.

With his encouragement to work out their salvation with fear and trembling the apostle wants to remind the Philippians, and all believers, that believers' lives in the world are a constant struggle. Daily a host of spiritual enemies, led by the devil and his scheming allies, seek to rob believers of their faith and of the eternal treasures the Lord has in store for them. To ward off these enemies and continue safely along the way to eternal life on which their Lord has placed them, believers must always be watchful and alert. They must fear and tremble at the thought of their own weakness and at the possibility that they, by spiritual laziness or carelessness, may foolishly throw their spiritual treasures

55

away. They must strenuously battle against their spiritual enemies to remain in faith.

The single most important element in this working and struggling is believers' diligent use of the means of grace, the gospel in word and sacrament. These means, by which the Holy Spirit first made them spiritually alive, are also the means by which he continues to work in believers' hearts to strengthen and nourish their faith and their spiritual lives. Believers who remain diligent and conscientious in using the means of grace will find in them all the spiritual strength necessary for the spiritual working of which the apostle speaks so urgently in our text.

The Lord's grace and strength, provided to believers in the means of grace, are the "power source" into which Christians must continually tap if they are to succeed in their spiritual struggles. This is emphasized once more by the apostle when he says, "for it is God who works in you to will and to act according to his good purpose." God's grace alone moves believers both to desire to serve God and to translate that desire into action. This is real encouragement for Christians. As they, with fear and trembling, turn to the Lord for help and strength to carry on the struggle of their Christian lives and retain their hold on their spiritual treasures, the Lord will not disappoint them. Through his word and sacraments he will continue to work in their hearts and supply all that they need to will and work for him. It is necessary for every Christian to be constantly plugged into the spiritual power source that God provides for us in his word and sacraments.

Willing and acting according to God's good purpose requires the correct attitude of the heart. Grudging obedience is not really obedience at all. So Paul urges, "Do everything without complaining or arguing." In the course of our lives as Christians we are often called on to do things that do not come naturally to us, things against which our selfish natures angrily rebel. We are often asked to do things which we know will bring scorn and ridicule from our non-Christian friends and associates. We are to do all these things, Paul says, without murmuring and complaint. There is to be no second-guessing of God, no grumbling about what God expects of us, no rationalizing or calculating about how we might escape our responsibilities or get by with doing less.

No parent is pleased when a child does as he is told, but grumbles throughout the entire task. That child makes it obvious that the task is not being done willingly. His heart is not in it. Christians' lives of obedience to the Lord should be, not just a matter of actions, but a matter of the heart. God does not want service or dollars or anything else from us without our hearts. Have you checked your attitude lately?

Christians who live their lives for their Lord from their hearts will be "blameless and pure, children of God without fault in a crooked and depraved generation." "Crooked and depraved" describes the world without Christ. Christians live in a world that has left the Lord's straight paths and become morally and spiritually warped, but they are to be different. Their conduct ought to be blameless before the world, their motives pure before God. As they live such pure and blameless lives, Christians will "shine like stars in the universe."

By God's grace the bright light of the gospel has dispelled the spiritual darkness that was by nature in Christians' hearts. Now God wants Christians, who have the light of life through Jesus, to be both light-reflectors and light-bearers in the sin-darkened world. As light-reflectors Christians should stand out from their worldly contemporaries as light shines in darkness. Their words and actions should cause people to see that believers belong to Christ and should lead those who observe them to glorify God.

Likewise, believers are to be light-bearers. They are to hold out the gospel light to those who are still in the darkness of spiritual ignorance and unbelief. What a pity that we Christians so often walk in the darkness of this world instead of bringing light to the darkness.

Finally, Paul gives his words of encouragement another very personal turn. In all they are, in all they do, in all he is encouraging them to be, he wants the Philippians to be a cause of boasting for him on judgment day. Paul enjoyed a warm and affectionate relationship with the members of the congregation at Philippi. He had founded the congregation and was still its spiritual counselor and friend. He loved the Philippians and found real joy in their response to the gospel. When he stands before the Lord on judgment day, he wants their lives to be evidences that his apostolic labors were not in vain. Paul had labored strenuously for the Philippians. What a wonderful testimony to the effectiveness of Paul's efforts their faith and Christian lives would be in the judgment.

Pastors, like Paul, experience many discouragements in their ministry. Sometimes it appears that their gospel teaching is falling on deaf ears. Sometimes their efforts to guide their hearers to God-pleasing Christian living meet with little apparent success. But eternity will reveal that the diligent efforts of faithful pastors and teachers were not in vain. What a wonderful relationship exists between a pastor and those he serves when the pastor can make, and the congregation will respond to, as deeply personal an appeal as the apostle makes here.

Earlier, in 1:25, Paul had indicated to the Philippians that he expected to be released from his imprisonment. That did

58

not change the fact, however, that he lived each day aware that his life could be required of him at any time. In connection with his personal appeal to the Philippians, therefore, he speaks of his possible martyrdom as "a drink offering on the sacrifice and service coming from your faith."

In the Old Testament rituals the drink offering was poured out next to the altar on which the burnt offering was sacrificed. Paul regarded believers' lives of obedience to the gospel as living sacrifices (see Romans 12:1) to the Lord. His own martyrdom, should it occur, would be a willing sacrifice on his part, a sacrifice poured out next to the sacrifices of the Christian lives of the Philippians. Far from hindering his labors on the Philippians' behalf, his martyrdom would crown those labors. Viewing it in that light the apostle could find joy even in the prospect of such a death, and he wanted the Philippians to find it, too. He wants believers of every age to be sharers of his joy.

Honor Your Gospel Servants

[19]I hope in the Lord Jesus to send Timothy to you soon, that I also may be cheered when I receive news about you. [20]I have no one else like him, who takes a genuine interest in your welfare. [21]For everyone looks out for his own interests, not those of Jesus Christ. [22]But you know that Timothy has proved himself, because as a son with his father he has served with me in the work of the gospel. [23]I hope, therefore, to send him as soon as I see how things go with me. [24]And I am confident in the Lord that I myself will come soon.

[25]But I think it is necessary to send back to you Epaphroditus, my brother, fellow worker and fellow soldier, who is also your messenger, whom you sent to take care of my needs. [26]For he longs for all of you and is distressed because you heard he was ill. [27]Indeed he was ill, and almost died. But God had mercy on him, and not on him only but also on me, to spare me sorrow upon sorrow. [28]Therefore I am all the more eager to send him, so that

when you see him again you may be glad and I may have less anxiety. ²⁹Welcome him in the Lord with great joy, and honor men like him, ³⁰because he almost died for the work of Christ, risking his life to make up for the help you could not give me.

Paul now returns to matters of a more personal nature. We recall that one of the reasons he wrote this epistle was to inform the concerned believers in Philippi about his well-being and the progress of his trial. Paul appreciated the special, personal concern the members of his beloved congregation had shown for him. He wanted them to know, too, that he was just as concerned about their welfare as they were about his. So he informed them that, just as soon as there was definite news about the outcome of his trial, he would dispatch a personal messenger to them. Paul earnestly hoped that would take place soon, and that the news would be good, but he left it all in the hands of the Lord whom he served, the Lord who would do what was best for him and for the Philippians.

For this special mission to the Philippians Paul had selected Timothy, his "right-hand man," whom he regarded as his own son. Timothy was probably the one man Paul could least afford to spare, but the apostle also knew that Timothy was the best qualified man for this particular task. Timothy shared the apostle's concerned and sympathetic spirit. He would understand why the apostle considered this mission so important, and he would carry it out in exactly the spirit Paul desired, so that it would bring real joy, encouragement, and mutual spiritual refreshment to the Philippians and the apostle.

Besides, the Philippians were well acquainted with Timothy. He had been with Paul when their congregation was founded and had become well acquainted with the Philippians. He felt the same cordial interest in their welfare as Paul did. Paul knew that the Philippian Christians would receive Timothy and exchange information with him freely and openly, as with a personal friend.

There were others with Paul in Rome who might have gone to Philippi for him, but he had eliminated everyone except Timothy. Some may have offered excuses. The apostle considered others spiritually immature or unqualified. Sadly he declared, "For everyone looks out for his own interests, not those of Jesus Christ."

There was apparently a lack of total commitment to Christ and his cause even among some of the apostle's co-workers. Some were unwilling to make real, personal sacrifices for Christ and his kingdom. Paul's rather harsh words here do not apply to all the other men who worked with him. Elsewhere he has high praise for men like Luke and Aristarchus. When these words were written, however, Luke and others were no doubt gone from Rome on other missions for the apostle. Paul was obviously disappointed in many of his co-workers that were with him just then in Rome. They wanted to be known as servants of Christ, but they refused to put Christ's work before their own interests.

This has always been a problem for the church on earth. Indeed, we are all sinners, and our service is not perfect. The apostle's words remind us again that real commitment to Christ means willingness to place the welfare of his kingdom before our own personal pleasures and preferences. It means willingness to place his interests before our own. Let us remember that the next time we are asked to perform some sacrificial service for our Lord and his church. In fact, let's remember it all the time.

The lack of commitment to the Lord that characterized many of his co-workers in Rome troubled Paul, but Timothy was different. Though he was still a relatively young man Timothy was spiritually mature. His faithfulness and reliability, even in difficult and dangerous situations, had been well established. Timothy was like a child who closely resembled Paul, his spiritual father. He shared Paul's total commitment to Jesus and the gospel. So Timothy was the man who would represent Paul well among the Philippians until the apostle himself could come to them. The Philippians were to receive and honor Timothy as they would have received and honored the apostle himself.

Paul goes on to speak of another co-worker who was well-known to the Philippians, Epaphroditus. He calls Epaphroditus a brother, united with him in faith, a fellow worker for the Gospel, and a fellow soldier, who has shared danger and hardship with the apostle in the struggle for the gospel. Epaphroditus, who was probably a leader in the church at Philippi, had been commissioned by the congregation to go to Rome, not only to take Paul a gift from their congregation, but to remain with Paul in Rome as his personal servant and assistant. Epaphroditus himself was actually a part of the gift that the Philippians sent to Paul. Paul regarded their sending of this man as a real spiritual service, something given not only to him but to the Lord.

Now, however, Paul was sending Epaphroditus back to the Philippians sooner than they had expected. In the course of serving the apostle, Epaphroditus had fallen ill. We are not told the nature of his illness. Perhaps the long journey, followed by strenuous efforts for the gospel and the apostle in Rome, had exhausted him. Perhaps he had fallen victim to malaria or to the fevers that often raged in Rome. At any rate Epaphroditus had been gravely ill. For a while, humanly speaking, his very life hung in the balance. In his mercy the Lord spared Epaphroditus' life, and, in that same mercy he spared the apostle the grief of having his faithful servant taken from him by death.

After Epaphroditus had recovered from his illness, Paul thought it best to send him back home to Philippi, for several reasons. The Philippians had heard about Epaphroditus' brush with death and were concerned about him. Epaphroditus, in turn, was concerned about their concern. He wanted to assure them that everything was fine again. Having only recently been at death's door, he was anxious to see and to be with his loved ones once more. So, to relieve Epaphroditus' anxiety and to ease the Philippians' concerns and bring them joy, Paul sent Epaphroditus back to them, no doubt carrying this very letter.

Once again Paul showed his unselfish concern for others. The needs of Epaphroditus and the Philippians meant more to him than the personal services he could still have received from Epaphroditus. If the Philippians and Epaphroditus were happy, then Paul would be happy, too. Paul had truly learned from Christ the secret of unselfish generosity and loving concern for others.

As he sends Epaphroditus back to them, Paul encourages the Philippians to welcome him warmly. There should be no criticism of the fact that his mission has been cut short. Epaphroditus has been a faithful servant. He has done all that he could. As those who had commissioned him, therefore, the Philippians should welcome him home joyfully and honor him for his faithfulness. As their servant as well as the apostle's, Epaphroditus has done what the rest of the Philippians could not do. He has personally gone in their place to serve the apostle in Rome, and in that service he has risked his very life. So, even though his mission may not have turned out exactly as anticipated, the Philippians owe Epaphroditus their gratitude and their respect.

Paul's encouragement to the Philippians to honor Epaphroditus as one who served in their stead encourages us, too, to honor those who serve for us. Our called pastors and teachers, as well as those who serve on boards and committees or voluntarily serve our congregations and the church at large in so many different ways, all represent us. They work in our place.

Think, too, of our world missionaries. Not many of us, and the writer of this volume here includes himself, possess the courage to leave family, friends and possessions behind and to start life anew in an unfamiliar land and culture to bring the gospel to lands in which it is not being proclaimed. Not many are able to endure all kinds of physical hardships and deprivations in order to share the good news of the Lord Jesus with those who would otherwise be lost. All the missionaries our church supports, together with their families, as well as the courageous nurses in our medical missions, have gone where they are and are doing what they are doing in your place and mine. Some of these mission workers will return in a relatively short period of time, for health or other reasons. Others spend whole lifetimes doing the Lord's work for us in faraway lands. We owe them all our respect, our gratitude, our prayers, our personal encouragement and our generous support.

Beware of Every Threat to Gospel Joy

3 **Finally, my brothers, rejoice in the Lord! It is no trouble for me to write the same things to you again, and it is a safeguard for you.**

2Watch out for those dogs, those men who do evil, those mutilators of the flesh. 3For it is we who are the circumcision, we who worship by the Spirit of God, who glory in Christ Jesus, and who put no confidence in the flesh — 4though I myself have reasons for such confidence.

If anyone else thinks he has reasons to put confidence in the flesh, I have more: [5]circumcised on the eighth day, of the people of Israel, of the tribe of Benjamin, a Hebrew of Hebrews; in regard to the law, a Pharisee; [6]as for zeal, persecuting the church; as for legalistic righteousness, faultless.

[7]But whatever was to my profit I now consider loss for the sake of Christ. [8]What is more, I consider everything a loss compared to the surpassing greatness of knowing Christ Jesus my Lord, for whose sake I have lost all things. I consider them rubbish, that I may gain Christ [9]and be found in him, not having a righteousness of my own that comes from the law, but that which is through faith in Christ — the righteousness that comes from God and is by faith. [10]I want to know Christ and the power of his resurrection and the fellowship of sharing in his sufferings, becoming like him in his death, [11]and so, somehow, to attain to the resurrection from the dead.

To introduce a new subject Paul returns to the key word of this epistle, "Rejoice." This time, however, he emphatically adds the words, "in the Lord." Paul wants the Philippians, whom he affectionately refers to as "my brothers," to find their real joy in the Lord alone and in their faith-union with him. He wants them to reject all teachings that would direct them to any other source of confidence or joy.

The subject Paul brings up here is not a new one. Earlier in the epistle (1:27) the apostle encouraged the Philippians to "stand firm in one spirit, contending . . . for the faith of the gospel." He had probably also spoken with them personally about this subject when he was with them. But in view of the serious threat that enemies of the gospel always pose to believers' salvation and to their joy in the Lord, Paul wanted to speak about this matter again. As a concerned shepherd and watchman of souls, Paul did not consider repeated warnings against false teachings a matter of "beating a dead horse." Rather, he considered such warnings beneficial, a spiritual safeguard for those he served.

With a three-fold "watch out" Paul warns against threats to the Philippians' spiritual safety. "Watch out for those dogs," he says, "those men who do evil, those mutilators of the flesh." The Philippian congregation was a fine congregation, but danger was theatening. Perhaps fresh news concerning the activity of certain false teachers in their area had just reached the apostle. At any rate he used very forceful and vigorous language here to condemn them. There is a vehemence here which is uncharacteristic of the rest of this primarily cheerful epistle. This does not surprise us. Paul always became excited when the gospel was at stake. This shows his deep love and concern for the souls of the believers whose spiritual needs he served.

Paul uses three different terms to refer to the enemies of the gospel against whom he is warning the Philippians here, but with all three he is actually referring to the same enemies, who are commonly called Judaizers. Judaizers were Jews or Gentile converts to Christianity who claimed to believe in Jesus as their Savior, but they also taught that in addition to believing in Jesus, it was necessary to keep certain ceremonial laws that God had given to the Old Testament Israelites through Moses.

The Judaizers placed special emphasis on the rite of circumcision, the Old Testament sign of God's covenant with Israel. By their insistence on the outward observance of laws and ceremonies as a necessity for salvation, in addition to faith, the Judaizers confused law and gospel. They attempted to rob New Testament believers of the freedom from the Old Testament laws and ceremonies that Jesus won for them (see also the comments on Colossians 2:16,17), and they continued to plant in human hearts the damnable idea that human beings can somehow make a contribution toward their own salvation. These Judaizers were a very real threat to the life and faith of the early church. They apparently established no congregations of their own, but they tried to worm their way into existing congregations. Paul wrote his epistle to the Galatians chiefly to combat the Judaizers' teachings. He also indicated that Judaizers were troubling the Corinthians.

The first recorded "synod meeting" of the New Testament church (Acts 15) exposed the errors the Judaizers were trying to promote in Antioch. The idea that Jesus' atoning work is not quite enough and human beings have to add something of their own to it is still spooking around in many Christian church bodies. It is no less of a problem than it was in the apostle's day. This human error continues to endanger faith and lead people away from Christ and salvation.

Paul applied harsh terms to the Judaizers, because they were attacking the very heart of the gospel. They were seeking to substitute for it a mixture of divine grace and human works. Dogs, Paul called the false teachers. That was a term that the Jews derisively hurled at the Gentiles, whom they regarded as unclean and lower than themselves. In the apostle's world dogs generally were not pets. They were large, ugly beasts that roamed the streets and lived on garbage. Paul took that insulting term that they so often applied to others and hurled it right back at the Judaizers.

The Judaizers were extremely proud of their "Jewishness" and the fact that they lived according to Jewish customs. But in reality, Paul says, it was the Judaizers who were the dogs. They were greedy scavengers who were bent on destroying Christ's church. Yes, the Judaizers were workers. They were busy and active. They worked hard at keeping the laws and regulations they insisted were necessary for salvation. Sadly, however, they were workers who did evil. Instead of helping the gospel's cause, their working harmed it.

We cannot help thinking here of many religious sects that exist and flourish today. Their zeal, enthusiasm and hard work put many of us to shame, but their false teachings condemn them as men and women who do evil.

In the original Greek the words "circumcision" and "mutilation" were very similar. The apostle, therefore, was using a play on words when he called these Judaizers "mutilators." The ritual of circumcision involved a physical cutting on the sexual organ of the male child. In the Old Testament this physical act was the outward, visible sign of Israel's special covenant relationship with the Lord.

In the New Testament, however, God no longer requires circumcision or any of the rituals of the ceremonial law. When Jesus died on Calvary and the temple veil was rent in two, all the ceremonial laws and regulations and their purpose came to an end. The Judaizers' insistence on circumcision, therefore, had no promise of God connected with it. They had reduced circumcision to an outward, physical ritual that supposedly contributed to salvation. Such a circumcision, Paul said, was really only a physical thing, a mutilation. Those who relied on it as a meritorious act were not brought closer to God. They were actually farther removed from God than before. If the Philippians yielded to the Judaizers' insistence that they had to be circumcised in order to be saved, they, too, would be trusting in their own wretched works to be saved, not in Jesus alone. If they did that, they would lose their salvation.

In the Old Testament those who were physically circumcised were members of the covenant people. In the New Testament age, however, God's covenant people, his "circumcised ones," are all those of every race and nation who truly believe in Jesus as their Savior and Lord. In the New Testament ethnic distinctions and outward signs like circumcision mean nothing. Faith in Jesus means everything. We believers are the circumcision, whether we are outwardly circumcised or not. Paul, the Philippian believers, all believers, you and I are God's New Testament children. We are those who have by faith received the "circumcision of the heart by the Spirit," as Paul tells the Romans. God's people in the New Testament age are those who glory in Christ and his cross and put no confidence in outward things like circumcision or other supposed human advantages.

Incidentally, Paul's words about the true New Testament people of God should help us answer the prominent religious figures of our day who insist that the Jews, *as a nation*, can still be identified with the kingdom of God and are still an integral part of God's plans for the salvation of mankind. From such unscriptural reasoning have followed many false conclusions, including the rather absurd notion that there are two "chosen nations" today, the United States and Israel, and that God has raised one up to protect the other. In the New Testament age the chosen people are all those in every nation who know and believe in Jesus as their Savior. They are not a physical nation who are identified by a special, visible mark on their bodies. They are a spiritual people.

To the Judaizers, fleshly things like ethnic background, physical rituals and outward displays of human endeavor meant everything. They labored under the perverted impression that their souls' salvation depended on those earthly things. Paul did not want the Philippians to be deceived by that kind of thinking. So he used his own life as an example of how perverted such thinking really is. If he chose

69

to argue with the Judaizers on their own terms, he would have greater reason for boasting than any Judaizer could ever have.

Were the Judaizers concerned about circumcision? Paul had been circumcised on the eighth day in strict accord with the ceremonial law. How many Judaizers, many of whom had been later converts to Christianity, could claim that? Were the Judaizers concerned about ethnic purity? Paul did not belong to a mixed stock of less than 100% pure Israelites, as most of the Jews after the Babylonian captivity did. He was a member of the tribe of Benjamin, one of only two tribes that had remained fairly intact after the Jews returned from exile. Paul was a Hebrew of Hebrews, a genuine Israelite through and through, with a genealogy that could put many of the Judaizers to shame.

His family had remained strictly faithful to the ancestral religion and even retained the Hebrew language, which many other Jews had forgotten. If the Judaizers were concerned about outward keeping of Old Testament ceremonial laws, Paul could boast that he had been a Pharisee, a member of the strict Jewish sect that prided itself in keeping the laws of Moses to the last detail. The Pharisees even added many of their own laws to the laws of Moses. Paul's father before him had been a Pharisee, and none of his contemporaries came close to being as good a Pharisee as Paul had been. During his years as a Pharisee Paul, then known as Saul, had diligently kept and upheld all the Pharisees' laws and regulations. His zeal for those laws, in fact, was so great that it had led him to try to violently destroy the infant Christian church, because it taught a way of salvation contrary to that which the Pharisees taught.

Measured by the standards of righteousness that the Judaizers upheld, therefore, Paul was practically faultless. And if heaven's gates could have been opened by any combination of these outward things, Paul, both by what he had inherited and what he had attained, would have been able to walk right in.

At one time, to Paul's spiritually blind eyes, all the things that he has just mentioned were "gain" to him. He considered them advantages that would help him gain eternal life. The Judaizers still thought that way. But, Paul said, by God's grace he had now been led to see all these outward things in their true light and to discover that they had no value at all. All those physical things, all those supposed advantages did not gain real righteousness for him. They only led him away from the only righteousness that saves.

The Lord had led Paul to that great discovery. One day, as Paul was on his way to Damascus to persecute the Christians there, the risen and ascended Lord Jesus appeared to him. In that moment Paul saw himself as the wretched, helpless sinner he really was. He experienced a complete change of heart and a total reversal of values. The Savior he had been persecuting became *his* Savior. The cause he had been bent on destroying became *his* cause. All the things that had been so precious to Saul the Pharisee became and remained forever useless to Paul the sinner saved by grace.

All these things he had formerly regarded as gain or profit he now regarded as less than useless, not because all of them were wrong in themselves, but because he had wrongly regarded them as tickets to eternal life. So, like a ship's captain tossing baggage off a foundering ship so that the ship would not sink, Paul ridded himself of all the things that had been so important to him. In that sense he lost everything. Yet in his heart he knew that his "loss" was really not loss at all. All the things he had discarded were nothing

71

but garbage, rubbish, a worthless mess, for they had stood in the way of his knowing and trusting in Christ.

In losing those earthly things as the object of his trust, Paul had through the Holy Spirit's work in his heart, gained Christ. During the thirty or so years that had elapsed between that experience on the Damascus road and the writing of this epistle, Paul's knowledge of Christ had grown and matured. The more he knew of his Savior and the more deeply he came to rest his confidence on him, the more that knowledge eclipsed everything else in beauty and desirability, as the apostle realized that nothing in all the world can be compared with knowing Christ.

It is important for us, too, to realize that some of the things we might regard as advantage or gain can actually be loss for us if they stand in the way of our knowing and trusting in Jesus. Being born into a Christian home, being instructed and confirmed, receiving a Christian education and being members of a Christian congregation are all great blessings and advantages in themselves, but we cannot regard them as tickets to eternal life. Likewise, other legitimate blessings of the Lord, like intelligence, money, charm and education, even our own personal moral victories, can actually become hindrances to our salvation, if for any reason we regard them as more important than knowing Christ or put our trust in them instead of placing our whole confidence in Christ.

Through Christ Paul obtained a righteousness that enables sinners to stand before the judgment seat of God. Before he came to know Jesus, Paul trusted the righteousness that he thought he was earning by the kind of life he led. But once the Scriptures were opened to him, the apostle came to realize how worthless all human righteousness really is.

Gaining one's own righteousness by keeping the law could be done only by perfectly fulfilling the law. In the law God demands perfect holiness in thought, desire, word and deed. No sinful human being can be perfectly holy. The righteousness that Paul thought he was earning as a Pharisee, the righteousness the Judaizers still claimed they and their pupils could earn, was worse than worthless.

In Christ, on the other hand, Paul had found real righteousness. Jesus earned this righteousness for sinners by his work as mankind's substitute. God freely gives that righteousness to sinners through the gospel. Individual sinners personally receive this righteousness by faith which the Holy Spirit kindles in their hearts through the very gospel message which announces and offers this righteousness. From beginning to end the righteousness that saves is God's free gift to sinners. On the basis of this righteousness alone God accepts sinful human beings as his children. Paul knew that in Christ he had obtained that marvelous righteousness from God. He was not about to give it up or foolishly place his trust again in the worthless human righteousness that had intrigued him before. Nor did he want the Philippians to be deceived by the Judaizers into giving it up.

Twenty centuries later the apostle's inspired words urge us, too, to place our confidence in the righteousness of Christ alone. The apostle encourages us to count everything else as loss for the surpassing greatness of knowing Christ and finding in him the righteousness that avails before God. He encourages us to reject all righteousness apart from Christ as sham righteousness which cannot save.

Believers, who possess Christ's righteousness and feel his love in their hearts, will, like the apostle, constantly want to grow in their knowledge of him. They will want to experience his love ever more deeply and respond to that love

73

with lives of loving service to Jesus. The Lord blesses such growth in his believers through the gospel in word and sacrament. As believers regularly find Christ in his word, remember their baptism, and receive Christ's body and blood in the Lord's Supper, the Holy Spirit reveals the Savior's beauty to them in ever clearer focus. He binds them ever more closely to that Savior, filling them more and more with the Savior's love and the desire and power to serve him. Through the Spirit's work in their hearts believers experience the power of Christ's resurrection. They receive from their risen Lord the spiritual strength to overcome sin and grow in Christian living.

They also experience, as Paul did, "the fellowship of sharing in his sufferings" and "becoming like him in his death." Believers cannot atone for their own sins by suffering and dying, but they share in the fellowship of Christ's suffering and become like him in his death when they endure the scorn and ridicule and even at times the physical persecution of the hostile world, when they daily crucify their own sinful and selfish nature with its lusts and desires, and when they joyfully and uncomplainingly follow their Savior on their path of suffering and trouble in this sinful world to the glory of eternal life with him. Toward that great goal Paul constantly strove; toward that great goal every believer, including each one of us, also daily strives.

Press Determinedly Onward to the Heavenly Goal

[12]Not that I have already obtained all this, or have already been made perfect, but I press on to take hold of that for which Christ Jesus took hold of me. [13]Brothers, I do not consider myself yet to have taken hold of it. But one thing I do: Forgetting what is behind and straining toward what is ahead, [14]I press on toward the goal to win the prize for which God has called me heavenward in Christ Jesus.

¹⁵All of us who are mature should take such a view of things. And if on some point you think differently, that too God will make clear to you. ¹⁶Only let us live up to what we have already attained.

¹⁷Join with others in following my example, brothers, and take note of those who live according to the pattern we gave you. ¹⁸For, as I have often told you before and now say again even with tears, many live as enemies of the cross of Christ. ¹⁹Their destiny is destruction, their God is their stomach, and their glory is in their shame. Their mind is on earthly things. ²⁰But our citizenship is in heaven. And we eagerly await a Savior from there, the Lord Jesus Christ, ²¹who, by the power that enables him to bring everything under his control, will transform our lowly bodies so that they will be like his glorious body.

4 Therefore, my brothers, you whom I love and long for, my joy and crown, that is how you should stand firm in the Lord, dear friends!

When believers are brought to faith, they become possessors of eternal life. As long as they are in the world, they are like people who hold title to property in a distant land. The title makes the property theirs, but the owners are not yet physically in possession of what rightfully belongs to them. Similarly believers, though they are possessors of eternal life by faith and have the righteousness of Christ, are still also sinners living in a sinful world. They have not yet arrived at the full, physical possession of the perfection of eternal life. So, perhaps in response to the boastful claims of the Judaizers or others who taught that believers by their works could achieve perfection already here on earth, Paul in this section vividly describes the Christian life as a constant straining forward toward the great goal and prize of eternal life that God's grace holds out to believers in Christ.

When Paul wrote these verses, he had been a Christian for many years. During those years he had grown in knowledge of Christ and in conformity to Christ. He had become a revered apostle and had experienced the fellowship of sharing in Christ's sufferings. Most recently he had suffered the loss of his personal freedom for the sake of Christ, but that did not mean that he had "arrived" spiritually or reached the goal of perfection. Paul was still living in a sinful world. He was still a sinner, still troubled by the weaknesses and failings of his sinful nature. Though he was a child of God by faith, he had not yet arrived at the point where he could perfectly and uninterruptedly serve God or enjoy the fullness of the blessings God had in store for him. That would have to wait until he entered heaven. Meanwhile he lived his life as a Christian in a constant striving for holiness. He pressed on toward perfection.

What Paul says of his own life here is an important key to viewing our own. As long as we are here on earth, we sinners will not reach perfection. That will come only in heaven's glory. Nevertheless, our Christian lives of growing in Christ and living for him ought to be a constant striving for perfection, with the goal and prize of eternal life kept ever before our eyes of faith.

The Greek and Roman worlds of the apostle's day shared our American fascination for sports. Archaeologists have unearthed ancient stadia as well equipped as many of our own. Paul uses the picture of the determined runner/athlete here in these verses to illustrate the intense yearning and striving for spiritual perfection that should characterize all believers as they "run the race" of their Christian lives. Success in athletic competition depends not only on ability and conditioning, but also on an athlete's mental state. Concentration is the key. Overconfidence, lack of mental alertness or "mental toughness" can cost an athlete dearly.

Spiritual dullness, overconfidence and lack of concentration can likewise cost Christians. Recall how Paul urged the Philippians in chapter 2:12 never to stop working at their salvation. The apostle is saying basically the same thing here in a slightly different way. The Christian who does not concentrate on living the kind of life to which God calls him may, like the overconfident athlete, be eliminated from the race and in the end lose the blessings God has in store for him. A believer's sanctification, that is, his life as a Christian in this world, will never be perfect. The struggle against sin and the devil must be carried on as long as the Christian is in this world. Neither Paul nor any other Christian can ever afford a lack of concentration or think that the race is as good as run and won.

The Apostle Paul concentrated and pressed on so that he could take hold of that for which Christ Jesus had taken hold of him. Paul was a believer because Christ had redeemed him with his blood and called him by the gospel to be his own. That call of the Savior included the promise of eternal joy. It also included the call for Paul to serve the Savior with his life. God's call to every believer includes that call to service here on earth, and in that call the Lord provides the spiritual power for such service. Motivated by the fact that Christ had reached out in grace and taken hold of him, Paul pressed onward with never-wavering concentration and all-out effort toward the blessed end to which Christ had promised that his life of faith would lead.

Twice in two verses Paul emphasizes the fact that he himself has not yet reached spiritual perfection or taken full possession of his eternal inheritance. This leads us to suspect that there were certain teachers who were confusing the Philippians with claims of perfection. Did some, perhaps the Judaizers, claim they could achieve perfection? Paul knew that he had not achieved it. When he viewed his life even as a Christian, he had to honestly admit, "What I do is not the good I want to do; no, the evil I do not want to do — this I keep on doing."

So Paul was not a perfectionist in the sense that he believed he had achieved perfection or could achieve it in his life on earth. That did not mean he became lazy or despaired or gave up striving for perfection. One writer called Paul an "untiring idealist." As we read his epistles, we see quite clearly that during his entire life as a Christian one holy passion filled the apostle's soul. He wanted to serve the Lord Jesus. He wanted to do it constantly. He strove to do it perfectly. He did not want anything to distract him from doing it. "One thing I do," he says, as he sums up that holy passion: "Forgetting what is behind, and straining toward what is ahead, I press on toward the heavenly goal to win the prize for which God has called me heavenward in Christ Jesus."

Looking back while running ahead is a dangerous procedure for the athlete in a race. It can only result in a loss of speed and direction. In the race of his Christian life the apostle did not look back either. He did not look back with pride on past accomplishments which he knew could not earn him anything in God's sight. Nor did he look back in regretful brooding over past sins which had been washed away by Jesus' blood. With each new day he put forth every effort to press ahead, to grow in his Christian living and service to Christ. The long distance runner strains and stretches every muscle, expending even more energy, if at all possible, as he draws closer to the finish line. Similarly, Paul was expending all the energy he possessed as a Christian, straining with all his spirtual might as he drew ever closer to the goal and the prize of eternal life.

78

Every Christian should run the race of his Christian life in that way. No, we won't reach perfection in our lives here on earth, because we are sinners, but there is no limit to the spiritual growth we can achieve by the grace and through the power of him who has called us to be his children and to serve him with our Christian lives.

At the end of the race course stood the goal. The winner of the race received the prize. For Christians the goal and the prize are the same thing: the end of our faith in the perfection of eternal life. When God calls Christians and brings them to faith, he sets that prize and goal before them. He encourages them always to keep that goal and prize in mind as they run the race of Christian life. For Christians, being called, running and reaching the goal are all "in Christ Jesus." Without Christ's atoning work for us, there would be no goal, no eternal prize. Without his Spirit's work in our hearts, we would neither run the race nor reach the goal, but in Christ and through faith in Christ we, the called ones, press on each day. We eagerly look forward to the day when we shall reach the end and goal of our faith and take full possession of that for which God has taken hold of us.

All mature believers should take this view of their lives. Understanding their own lack of perfection, they should, in Christ, never stop striving for perfection. They should never lose sight of the eternal goal that the Lord has set before them. These are the general principles that should govern believers' lives.

At times, of course, there may be disagreement as to the exact manner in which those principles should be applied. Christians will not always agree on how Christian love should properly be applied in situations where the word of God has not spoken. The Bible, after all, is not a code book with rules for every situation, but it does clearly set down all the general principles that Christians need to direct their lives as they press forward to their eternal goal. As they together seek to apply those principles in a loving way to various practical situations, the Lord will help them agree on how they should act. And, of course, Christians should always act in accord with the knowledge and spiritual maturity they have attained.

It was important that the Philippians take note of the principles of Christian living that Paul, with such care, explains to them here. It was also important for them to choose the right kind of examples to follow as they worked to put these principles into practice. With great affection, and deeply moved by the warning he is now compelled to give, Paul pleads, "Brothers, let me be your example."

By offering himself as an example, a role model for the Philippians, Paul was not boasting. In 1 Corinthians 11:1 he says, "Follow my example, as I follow the example of Christ." The Philippians recognized Paul, Timothy and others as spiritually mature believers, whom the Lord himself had qualified to serve as their examples. Paul understood (see also 1 Timothy 3) that setting a good example was a necessary part of his calling as an apostle and a pastor. Both Paul and the Philippians realized that, because they were surrounded by pagan immorality and by false teachers who wanted to deceive them, they needed good examples. So in genuine concern Paul pleads with them to follow his apostolic example. We would also do well to ask ourselves what kind of examples we follow, and what kind of examples we set for others.

Earlier Paul had warned the Philippians about the Judaizers, who taught that certain works which they regarded as particularly holy and righteous had to be added to faith. Now he warns against certain "enemies of the cross" who went to the opposite extreme. Apparently they too claimed to be Christians, but their openly wicked and sensual life-style belied the confession of their lips. To them "Christian freedom" from laws and restrictions such as the Judaizers wanted to impose could also be extended to mean freedom from all laws, including God's unchangeable moral will.

This philosophy was no doubt quite appealing to newly converted Christians who had been so used to the immoral life-styles of the pagan world. Already when he had personally been with them, Paul had warned the Philippians against this kind of lawless teaching. Now he warns them again. Indeed, because of his deep love and concern for their spiritual welfare, he warns them with tears against those who call themselves Christians but stand for everything that is opposed to Christianity.

Friends of Jesus' cross show by their lives that they have caught the spirit of the cross. Their lives are characterized by unselfishness, humility, and the unceasing desire to know Christ more deeply and to imitate him more fully. Enemies of the cross are those who substitute selfishness and self-indulgence for love and humility and who live their lives only to satisfy themselves. "Their god is their stomach," Paul says, "their glory is in their shame. Their mind is on earthly things." "Stomach," as the apostle used the term here, represents all the desires and appetites of the sinful nature: greed, gluttony, drunkenness, sexual immorality and anything else that satisfies what the sinful nature demands.

Instead of working to control their perverse appetites, these pseudo-Christians surrendered themselves to those appetites. By regarding the satisfaction of their fleshly, sinful desires as the most important thing in their lives, they actually made their desires their gods. Far from being ashamed of the kind of lives they were leading, they boasted about them, even going so far as to claim that such living was consistent with their Christian confession. The apostle dismisses all such twisted claims with one terse phrase: "Their destiny," often their earthly destiny, but above all their eternal destiny, "is destruction."

Twentieth century Christians can readily identify with the apostle's warning here. Like the Philippians, Christians today are besieged with the lofty-sounding claims of modern, worldly-minded "Christians" who urge us to follow their example. Some who call themselves Christian and are acclaimed as church leaders shamelessly accommodate themselves to the thinking of the world and the satisfaction of their fleshly desires. Enemies of the cross, they not only defend, but openly and boastfully advocate sins like adultery, homosexuality, abortion — although the Bible expressly condemns such things as abominations in God's sight. They haughtily proclaim biblical morality to be irrelevant and out of date.

Even more dangerous are those "Christians" who show by their lives that they have made worldly things like money, possessions and pleasure their gods. It is not very difficult even for those who really believe they are loyal followers of Jesus to become enemies of the cross in that way. We all need the tear-filled warning the apostle sounds here. We need to regard all those temptations to live for ourselves and not for our Savior with the apostle's sobering reminder ringing in our ears: "Their destiny is destruction."

The enemies of the cross live for this world and its pleasures and sins. They are earth-bound and world-oriented. Such concerns, however, ill befit Christians, who live in this world but are not permanent citizens of the world. Our citizenship, Paul reminds the Philippian Christians, is in heaven. Although they lived far from the imperial city of Rome, the Philippians were proud of their Roman citizenship. They cherished the special privileges that citizenship gave to them. They thought of Rome as their native land, the place where they really belonged. They knew their names were enrolled in the tribal records there. They dressed as Romans, spoke the language of Rome and enjoyed Rome's protection.

In a far more sublime and important sense, Paul tells the Philippians, they should realize that their most important citizenship, their spiritual citizenship, is in heaven. Heaven is the real home of believers. Their rights have been secured in heaven, and their interests are being promoted there. Their names are recorded in heaven's book of life. To heaven their prayers ascend and their hopes aspire. Many of their friends in Christ are already enjoying their full inheritance in heaven, and one day all believers will take up permanent residence there.

Their heavenly citizenship should be reflected in the way believers live their lives here on earth. Citizens of heaven should not regard this world as a place to put down permanent roots, nor should they fix their hearts on the things of this world or regard them as permanent possessions. They should consider themselves strangers and pilgrims on earth, and their greatest concern should be with heavenly, spiritual things.

From heaven, Paul joyfully concludes, we eagerly await the Savior, who will return to give us the physical possession of our eternal inheritance there. As heavenly-minded believers, we do not want to waste our time in pursuing earthly advantages and worldly pleasures. We do not want to let earthly concerns blind us to the importance of our heavenly citizenship. We want to use the time the Lord gives us on earth to prepare ourselves for the Savior's return and our entry into the glory of heaven.

Heavenly-minded believers never forget that Jesus, the Savior who once came in lowliness to save the world, is coming again in majesty and glory to judge the world. They await that return, not with fear or spiritual carelessness, but with expectant joy. When Jesus returns, not only believers' souls, but also their bodies will share in his eternal glory.

For the third time in three chapters Paul mentions the resurrection of the body. When Jesus returns, he will transform believers' lowly bodies and make them like his own glorious body. In 1 Corinthians 15 Paul tells us that the bodies of believers still alive at Christ's return will be changed, and the bodies of those who have died in the Lord will be raised and glorified.

The pagan philosophers of the first century regarded the body as an evil prison from which the soul would some day be delivered. Philosophers of every age have scoffed at the Christian teaching of the resurrection of the body, but Christians believe that the body is God's creation and their bodies are God's temples. Because of sin our bodies now are lowly bodies. In those bodies we experience all the weakness and frailty that are the consequences of sin. At the time of physical death the body of weakness is separated from the soul and eventually decays in the grave.

At his reappearing our Savior will raise all the dead. He will transform believers' bodies, so that they will reflect the perfect blessedness of their glorified souls. In the resurrection Jesus will make believers' bodies like his own glorified body. All sinfulness, weakness and the consequences of sin will be forever purged away. Believers' bodies and souls will be reunited to live forever in a perfect eternity in heaven with Christ.

Our human minds cannot imagine how the Lord will find the bodies which for thousands of years have been disposed of in so many different ways and subjected to the ravages of decay. Nor does the Apostle Paul try to satisfy our intellectual curiosity about these things. He tells us all we need to know when he simply says that Jesus will accomplish this marvelous feat through his almighty power, the power that enables him to bring the whole universe under his control.

What tremendous comfort these inspired words bring us as we stand grieving at the graves of loved ones who have died in the Lord. What a powerful encouragement they provide for us to continue to serve the Lord with our bodies as we press eagerly forward to the goal of the resurrection of the body and the life everlasting.

Paul deeply loved the Philippian congregation. Its members brought special joy to his heart, because the fruits of their faith were evident in so many ways in their lives. They were his crown, his festive garland. This was true when Paul wrote this epistle, but it would become even more evident at the Lord's return. Then their faith and the fruits of their faith would be displayed before the whole world as evidences that the apostle's labors were not in vain. Paul warmly reminds the Philippians of all this as he concludes this section. He re-emphasizes the importance of all he has just said, as he emphatically proclaims, "That is how you should stand firm in the Lord, dear friends!"

Let the Peace of the Gospel Be Evident in Your Lives

[2]**I plead with Euodia and I plead with Syntyche to agree with each other in the Lord.** [3]**Yes, and I ask you, loyal yokefellow, help these women who have contended at my side in the cause of the gospel, along with Clement and the rest of my fellow workers, whose names are in the book of life.**

⁴Rejoice in the Lord always. I will say it again: Rejoice! ⁵Let your gentleness be evident to all. The Lord is near. ⁶Do not be anxious about anything, but in everything, by prayer and petition with thanksgiving, present your requests to God. ⁷And the peace of God, which transcends all understanding, will guard your hearts and your minds in Christ Jesus.

⁸Finally, brothers, whatever is true, whatever is noble, whatever is right, whatever is pure, whatever is lovely, whatever is admirable — if anything is excellent or praiseworthy — think about such things. ⁹Whatever you have learned or received or heard from me, or seen in me — put it into practice. And the God of peace will be with you.

Their hopes for the return of the Lord and the glory of the world to come do not make Christians indifferent to this life and its problems and duties. Rather, they help them to see life in a clearer perspective. The light of Christ's coming falls on the present and fills it, despite all its dangers and difficulties, with joy and peace. Paul wanted the Philippians — and he wants us — to experience that joy and peace in the various situations of life.

The apostle's first admonition in this last short series of encouragements will surely bring a knowing smile or, more likely, a sigh, to pastors in just about every congregation. Here on earth, also in the visible Christian church, we are all sinners, living and working with sinners, and sooner or later sin is going to affect our interpersonal relationships. In the carrying out of the congregation's activities, or in the course of activity in its organizations, sinful human beings with strong opinions and forceful personalities are inevitably going to clash. Something very minor might be the trigger. Sharp words are spoken. Feelings are hurt. Grudges are held. The result is lingering bitterness, even factions that can truly disturb a congregation and hinder its witness and its work.

We are not given the details, but something quite similar to what is described above had taken place in Philippi. Two prominent women in the congregation, Euodia and Syntyche, had become involved in a dispute. We know nothing more about either of these women. Evidently they had served harmoniously and enthusiastically as co-workers of Paul, helping to aid the gospel ministry. Apparently they had both continued to be active in the congregation after Paul left Philippi. Both were energetic and talented. Both had been a rich source of blessing to the congregation. Now, however, some disagreement had arisen between them — a result of jealousy, perhaps? — and where there had been harmony before, there was now strife. The exact effect of the dispute on the congregation and its work is not stated, but we can be sure that it was not positive.

Paul handles this delicate situation with a marvelous combination of tact and Christian love. He does not question the motives of either of the women or their commitment to the Lord. He does not open old wounds by going into a lengthy rehashing of the problem. He does not scold or fix blame. He is not negative at all. He simply pleads with each of the women to agree with one another "in the Lord," whom they were both eager to serve. Note the even-handedness displayed in Paul's words of encouragement. He repeats the phrase "I plead," using first the name of one, then the name of the other woman as the object. He encourages each one to reflect on the blessings she had received from the Lord and to realize that this disagreement was not furthering Christ's cause in Philippi. He expresses the hope that mature Christian reflection on this matter will lead them both to expend their talents and energies in unity and for the Lord rather than in competition and disagreement.

Throughout this epistle Paul has emphasized the importance of unity and harmony among believers. Remembering the importance of that unity would help Euodia and Syntyche settle their dispute. And is it not true that the disputes over external things that often arise in our congregations today would also be settled more easily if we always remembered that as believers we are united in a blessed partnership in the gospel of Christ? We are working for a common task which could be hindered by our petty and sinful squabbles. Let's not forget either that we are destined to spend eternity together.

In addition to making his personal pleas to each of the women, Paul asks the aid of another of the congregation's members in mediating the dispute. There is some question about whether the Greek word *syzygus*, which means yokefellow, is a proper or a common noun here. I am inclined to believe that Paul is here addressing a man named Syzygus and asking him to be true to his name by helping to bring about a reconciliation between the two women.

Whether his proper name was Syzygus or not, this "yokefellow" was obviously a respected leader in the congregation. Paul knew he possessed the tact and love required for this important task. The apostle was anxious to see peace restored between Euodia and Syntyche. Every time he thought of them, he remembered the extraordinary efforts both had put forth for the sake of the gospel, together with him, Clement and others at Philippi. It did not seem right to have these two fine Christian women at odds with each other. He was hopeful that, with the right kind of assistance and encouragement, the problem would soon be solved.

From his specific admonition to Euodia and Syntyche Paul returns to a more general encouragement. Sounding the keynote of this epistle once more, he describes the spirit that should fill the hearts of the Philippians and all believers all the time. "Rejoice in the Lord!" Paul says. This time he adds *always*. Like sunshine, the purest, highest joy should always shine forth from Christians' lives. Joy should be a fundamental mark of every believer's personality. Because it does not always seem reasonable to rejoice, especially when believers are facing trying and difficult circumstances, the apostle repeats his encouragement, "I will say it again: "Rejoice!"

Can believers really feel joy in their hearts when they are troubled by past sins? Can they rejoice when they or those whom they love are facing life's sharp edges of unemployment, financial problems, sickness, uncertainty, pain and death? Remember Paul wrote these words as a prisoner, a man with years behind him of being "conformed to the fellowship of Christ's suffering" and an uncertain future ahead of him. Yet he wrote this epistle with a song in his heart and words of praise on his lips.

The apostle's obvious lesson, then, is that outward circumstances do not and should not determine the condition of a believer's heart. Even when everything around them is dark and gloomy, Christians can be joyful within. They can be joyful because of their oneness with Christ. Christ's Spirit fills believers' hearts continually with real gospel joy: the joy of forgiveness, the joy of knowing that in all things God works for the good of those who love him, the joyful assurance that Jesus is coming again to give us the full physical possession of our eternal inheritance in glory. If we call these unshakeable gospel assurances to mind each day, we shall understand that it is far from unreasonable for the apostle to urge us to rejoice in the Lord always. Nor is it unreasonable for us to urge one another always to rejoice.

In my calling as a pastor and caretaker of souls I have used this encouragement of the apostle to bring comfort to the sick, the shut-in and the dying. I have used it to encourage those who are depressed and downtrodden by earthly troubles and difficulties that never seem to end. I have used it as a text for a funeral sermon, and I have been comforted by it when I personally sat in a mourner's pew. How precious these encouraging words of the apostle are. Oh that all of us would heed this encouragement and, ever remembering the incomparable spiritual treasures we possess in Christ, rejoice in the Lord — always!

Joyful Christians also feel within themselves a compelling need to share joy. The joy in their hearts will become evident by a gentleness in their conduct. "Gentleness" is the translation that has been selected here for a Greek word that cannot really be reproduced by a single word in English. Expressions that come close to reflecting its meaning are "bigheartedness" and "sweet reasonableness."

What Paul is saying here is that Christians ought to be people who would much rather suffer wrong than inflict it. Gentleness or sweet reasonableness is another of those distinguishing characteristics that ought to mark Christians as different, special people in this world, people with a self-sacrificing attitude that imitates the humility of Christ. Where others loudly demand their rights, believers will gladly yield theirs. They will make the interests of the weak and helpless their concern and patiently yield to others, wherever such yielding does not violate their Christian principles.

In this area, too, all of us have much growing to do. Gentleness is not always evident in our Christian homes, much less in our relationships to our neighbors in the world. We need the Holy Spirit's constant help and blessing to give evidence of our Christian joy in gentle treatment of others.

The nearness of Christ's return should also be an encouragement to joy within and gentleness without. The early Christians were deeply conscious of the fact that each passing day brought them closer to Christ's return. Frequently they greeted each other with the word *maranatha*, which means, "Come, Lord Jesus."

Over 19 centuries have passed since Paul wrote, "The Lord is near." By God's way of reckoning, Christ is still near. For individual believers Christ's summons from this life to eternity is near. It could come at any time. So could Christ's return in glory. If we understand that, we shall want to live in the same eager, expectant spirit of rejoicing in which those early believers lived. How small a thing the sacrificing of some earthly rights becomes when we know that all wrongs will be righted when Christ appears. How meaningless the selfish lives of the unspiritual people around us appear. How significant lives of gentle joyfulness become.

Consciousness of the Lord's return will also help believers put into practice the apostle's next encouragement, "Don't be anxious about anything." There is, of course, such a thing as God-pleasing, kindly concern and genuine interest in the welfare of others. What the apostle discourages here is worry and anxiety about those things over which we have no control. We human beings are a worrying people. We worry about food and clothing, about what the future will bring, and about many other things. But worry is a sin. It shows a lack of trust in God. Do not be anxious and worried, Paul tells us. In childlike trust, leave everything in the Lord's loving hands.

The Lord does not forbid us to make plans or to think ahead. He does not want us to regard prayer as a substitute for planning and working. He wants us to use forethought and common sense to meet the various challenges and problems he sets before us in life, but in all our working and planning and thinking ahead, we Christians dare never forget that the outcome depends completely on the Lord's will and on his blessing.

With childlike trust, therefore, we should commend ourselves and our concerns to the Lord in prayer. The Lord knows our needs without our praying about them, but he lovingly invites and encourages us to bring them all to him in prayer. Into what more capable hands could we place them? And he actually promises that he will be moved by our prayers. It's our loss if we don't pray. "O what peace we often forfeit," the hymn writer reminds us, "O what needless pain we bear, all because we do not carry everything to God in prayer."

Nor should our prayers be restricted only to requests. If they are, we are praying selfishly. Christians' prayers should also include thanksgiving. Paul began every one of his epistles with outpourings of thanksgiving to God, and throughout his writings he continually emphasizes the importance of giving thanks. A prayer without thanksgiving is like a bird without wings. It has trouble rising upward.

Above all these encouragements Paul places in bold letters a wonderful promise. Over all of believers' lives, over all their labors and endeavors, rests the blessed peace of God. The peace of God originates in God. In love he imparts that peace to his children, his believers. He fills their hearts with peace through the gospel assurance that in Christ Jesus their sins are forgiven and they are at peace with him.

Peace and grace are often mentioned by the apostle in the same breath because peace results from grace. The peace of God has been called "the smile of God reflected in the soul of the believer." That precious peace, which passes all understanding, Paul assures his readers, will guard their hearts and minds in Christ Jesus.

The Philippians were used to the sight of Roman sentries standing guard. In that way, the apostle tells them, God's peace stands guard at the door of the believer's heart. God's peace standing guard keeps believers steadfastly clinging to Christ. It prevents care from wearing on their hearts and keeps unworthy thoughts from disturbing them. By trust and prayer believers enter the impregnable fortress of God's peace in the Lord Jesus Christ, a fortress from which nothing can dislodge them.

Finally, Paul says, Christians guarded by God's peace should endeavor to cultivate a wholesome thought-life. Their thoughts should center on all those virtues that are pleasing to God, and they should strive to put them into practice in their lives. Here, too, we reap what we sow. The kind of thought-life we cultivate will be reflected in the kind of words and actions we produce. So Christians must daily endeavor to fill their minds with things that are truthful and not vain or deceptive. They should think about things that are respectable and befitting Christian dignity, things that agree with God's law, things that are moral and pure, things that breathe and evoke the spirit of Christian love, things that are excellent and worthy of praise before both God and man.

Are we concerned enough about the kind of thought-life we are cultivating as Christians? Are the things with which we regularly fill our minds really the things that are true and noble, right and pure, lovely and admirable, excellent and praiseworthy? Or are we in the habit of filling our minds with the moral garbage on which our ungodly society gorges itself? Do the books we read, the television programs we watch, the movies we see, even the things we have trained our minds and eyes to catch as we go about our daily routine in life contribute to a wholesome thought-life? Or are we allowing our thought-lives to become greenhouses in which the devil's plants are grown? What we sow in our thought-lives, we reap in our words and actions. "Brothers, think on these things."

Paul and others had clearly taught the Philippians about the excellent and praiseworthy things that Christians should think about, and they had exemplified them in their conduct. The Philippians knew that Paul was not a pastor who said, "Do as I say, not as I do." He was a pastor whose word and example they could joyfully heed and follow. As the Philippian believers heeded his instructions and followed his example, as Christians of every age heed the instructions and follow the examples of faithful pastors and teachers, they will enjoy the presence of the God of peace in their lives as their guide and helper, encourager and friend.

THANKS AND GREETINGS
PHILIPPIANS 4:10-23

Joyful Thanks for a Gift of Love

[10]I rejoice greatly in the Lord that at last you have renewed your concern for me. Indeed, you have been concerned, but you had no opportunity to show it. [11]I am not saying this because I am in need, for I have learned to be content whatever the circumstances. [12]I know what it is to be in need, and I know what it is to have plenty. I have learned the secret of being content in any and every situation, whether well-fed or hungry, whether living in plenty or in want. [13]I can do everything through him who gives me strength.

[14]Yet it was good of you to share in my troubles. [15]Moreover, as you Philippians know, in the early days of your acquaintance with the gospel, when I set out from Macedonia, not one church shared with me in the matter of giving and receiving, except you only; [16]for even when I was in Thessalonica, you sent me aid again and again when I was in need. [17]Not that I am looking for a gift, but I am looking for what may be credited to your account. [18]I have received full payment and even more; I am amply supplied, now that I have received from Epaphroditus the gifts you sent. They are a fragrant offering, an acceptable sacrifice, pleasing to God. [19]And my God will meet all your needs according to his glorious riches in Christ Jesus.

[20]To our God and Father be glory for ever and ever. Amen.

Too many people in our busy society do not take the time to practice the courtesy of acknowledging gifts. The Apostle Paul was not like that. Although it was not his chief purpose, part of his purpose in writing to the Philippians was to acknowledge a gift, probably a gift of money, that they had sent to him at Rome, and to thank them for it. No doubt the apostle had sent the Philippians a verbal acknowledgement, perhaps with someone who was traveling from Rome to Philippi, as soon as he had received the gift. Now he takes the time to write his thanks. He states what the gift really means to him, and he tells of the uniquely Christian reason for which he appreciates it.

From the time they had first become acquainted with Paul, the Philippians, more than any other congregation of Christians, showed a special, personal interest in the apostle's physical welfare. Now once more, like a tree that puts forth new shoots each spring, the Philippians' concern for him had found a way of expressing itself. As soon as they had learned about his imprisonment, the Philippians had wanted to do something to help the apostle.

For a time, however, they were unable to carry out their resolve. Something had hindered them. Perhaps the grinding poverty that had affected the entire region some years earlier (see 2 Corinthians 8:12) was still making life economically difficult for the Philippians, or perhaps no messenger was immediately available to make the long journey to Rome. At any rate, the obstacles that had previously prevented the Philippians from expressing their generosity had now been removed, and Epaphroditus had brought a generous gift to the apostle on the Philippians' behalf. He was now returning to Philippi with this letter and with the apostle's warm thanks.

When Paul received the gift from the Philippians, he "rejoiced greatly in the Lord." Here Paul uses that key word "rejoice" for the last time in the epistle. We can well imagine what a special joy receiving this gift brought to Paul. After a long and dangerous sea voyage he had arrived at Rome as a prisoner. In a huge city he had never visited before he had to go about the task of preparing a legal defense to present to the highest court in the empire. He knew that if that defense failed, it could cost him his life.

What a joyful surprise it was when a trusted friend, Epaphroditus, arrived from his beloved Philippian congregation to serve as his personal attendant in Rome, to bring a gift from the congregation and, most important of all, to cheer the apostle with the assurance that his friends in Philippi had not forgotten him. Paul was an emotional man, and he was deeply moved by the Philippians' kind gesture.

Paul was deeply grateful to the Philippians for their thoughts of him and for their gift, and he was lavish in his thanks. Still, ever the teacher, he did not want to give the Philippians a wrong impression. He did not want them to think that earthly things had suddenly become overwhelmingly important to him. Nor did he want them to think that the Lord had left him in desperate physical straits or that his warm thanks was nothing more than a veiled plea for another gift. He wanted the Philippians to pause with him and see this gift of theirs in its proper perspective. He wanted them to know that there were certain things about their giving of the gift that were even more important than the gift itself.

Regardless of his physical circumstances, Paul tells his readers, he has learned always to be content. Throughout his lifetime, and especially during his years as an apostle, Paul experienced earthly circumstances that varied from great need to great plenty. At times the Lord granted him periods of rest and refreshment, even relative prosperity, but more often the apostle had lived in less than prosperous circumstances. As he served the Lord — often, in fact, *because* he served the Lord — he suffered hunger, cold, nakedness, beatings, imprisonment and lack of the physical comforts many others would have considered necessities.

No matter what physical circumstances he faced, Paul had learned the secret of being truly satisfied. He had found that secret in Christ. Daily, as Christ came to him in his word and as he came to Christ in prayer, the apostle found a source of strength and a never-failing fountain of contentment that could lead him confidently to declare, "I can do everything through him [namely Christ] who gives me strength."

Whatever needed to be faced or done or accomplished or suffered, Paul was confident that he could meet the challenge because he by faith was "in Christ." Christ's grace was sufficient for him. Christ's power rested on him. Christ himself stood by him, supplying his every need. Whatever physical things the Lord chose to give to him or withhold from him, and no matter how the Lord worked in his life, Paul was content, because he knew the Lord Jesus was on his side.

We, too, can be content with whatever the Lord gives us, be it little or much. We, too, have the assurance that, because we are in Christ by faith, he is always there beside us to give us the strength he knows we need to cope with life in the world and to live our lives for him. Many Christian families have attractive plaques hanging in their homes inscribed with the words: "I can do all things through Christ which strengtheneth me." There was one in my boyhood home. What a good reminder those words are for each Christian everyday. What a wonderful assurance they provide, an assurance that grows more precious and meaningful with every passing year.

Having taught the lesson, Paul now returns to his thank you. He wants the Philippians to know that he was pleased with the gift and that he appreciated it. Note how he does it. He does not just say, "Thanks for the gift. I am glad about it, because I can surely use it." He says, "Thank you for the gift. I am glad about it, because of what it says to me about you."

Their giving him this gift, the apostle tells the Philippians, was a beautiful deed. In deciding to give it, the Philippians had felt the apostle's afflictions as if they were their own. This was not the first time the Philippians had shown such extraordinary generosity. Paul vividly remembered that, soon after their congregation was founded, they had sent him a gift to assist him in his ministry at Thessalonica, the very next stop on his second mission journey. The congregation had been and still was a particularly generous congregation.

As generous as their gifts to him were, however, Paul reminds the Philippians that the truly important thing about any gift is not the gift itself, but the heart of the giver. It was above all because they had given their gift in the right spirit that Paul was overjoyed. The Philippians enjoyed a blessed giving and receiving relationship with the Apostle Paul. He had given them the gospel, and they had gladly received it. They, on their part, had shown their gratitude for the gospel by providing the apostle with material gifts that the Lord used to support and sustain him in his ministry. On their side of the giving and receiving ledger stood a clear and beautiful testimony to their generosity. Paul knew that the Lord would graciously reward that generosity, as he always does, even though believers don't give for the sake of a reward (see Proverbs 11:17, Malachi 3:10-12, 2 Corinthians 9:7, Luke 6:38).

As for himself, Paul says, his needs have been amply supplied. He rejoiced because he recognized the Philippians' generosity as a fruit of their faith. The Lord was also pleased with their gifts. He regarded them like the sweet-smelling incense offered to him by the Old Testament believers. Our gifts, too, are like sweet-smelling offerings to the Lord if —but only if — they are given out of hearts filled with genuine faith and love for him.

Just as they have so generously given to supply his needs, Paul assures the Philippians that God, who used their generosity to bless him, would, in turn, bless them by satisfying all their needs. He will do it "according to his riches in Christ Jesus." Those who are his children in Christ Jesus are the special objects of God's providence and loving care. They have the promise that he will never leave them or forsake them. He will supply their needs, not simply out of his glorious riches, as a millionaire throws coins to a beggar, but richly and daily "in accord with" the all-surpassing riches of the one to whom the whole universe belongs.

Reflecting on all of the things for which he himself can thank the Lord, as well as on the blessings and the care that the Lord bestows on all his children, Paul breaks forth in a final song of praise, glorifying God. To this great God, who in Christ Jesus is the believers' Father in a special way, the apostle ascribes adoration and praise. He calls for all believers to join him in a constant, never-ending song of praise. And his solemn Amen underscores the truth that this song of praise is a spontaneous expression of a heart redeemed by grace.

Final Greetings

21 Greet all the saints in Christ Jesus. The brothers who are with me send greetings. 22 All the saints send you greetings, especially those who belong to Caesar's household.

23 The grace of the Lord Jesus Christ be with your spirit.

With the song of praise in verse 20 Paul closes the body of his letter. All that remains now are the greetings. It is quite possible that Paul wrote these last verses with his own hand. A secretary probably wrote the rest. All the saints, that is, all the people who by grace have been set apart as God's children in Philippi, are given greetings, both from Paul and from the co-workers that were with him in Rome. Even though Paul has expressed disappointment with some of those co-workers (see 2:20), he does not exclude them from this greeting.

The circle of greeters widens to include all the believers in Rome. They all want to send their good wishes and express their unity in Christ. Those who belong to Caesar's household receive special mention. These Christians may have been government officials, perhaps even some members of the palace guard (see 1:13). The reason for their special mention here may be that, since Paul was involved in an imperial court case, these were the Christians with whom he had the closest contact at the time he wrote this epistle. Or perhaps since Philippi was a Roman colony, some of these officials personally knew or were even related to some of the Philippian believers. What is important to note once more is that Christianity had entered even the ranks of the highest Roman officialdom. Those believers, too, wanted to encourage the Philippians with their greetings.

Paul closes with a benediction, pronouncing the grace of God on his readers. We can picture to ourselves the scene in which the letter brought by Epaphroditus to the overseers and deacons at Philippi was read to the congregation assembled for worship. On them, and on all who might read this letter in the future Paul, the Lord's apostle, pronounces the blessing of God's grace. Thus he once more reminds us that what makes us Christians is the undeserved love of God to us poor sinners in Jesus the Savior. On that blessing hinge all our other blessings as Christians and all the things the apostle has written in this wonderful epistle of joy. Through that grace of God we, too, have an unshakeable peace and joy.

The grace of the Lord Jesus be with your spirit.

COLOSSIANS
INTRODUCTION

Only two of the thirteen New Testament letters authored by the Apostle Paul were addressed to congregations he had not founded and most of whose members he had never met. One was Romans, the other Colossians. In Colossians 2:1 Paul speaks of believers in that city "who have not met me personally." There was, however, a close connection between the apostle and the Colossian congregation. On his third mission journey Paul spent three entire years in Ephesus, the capital of the Roman province in which Colosse was located. During those three years people from all over the province came to Ephesus to hear the gospel from Paul. At the same time, Paul's co-workers and converts were very active in carrying the gospel from Ephesus to cities throughout the area. Undoubtedly, Colosse was one of the many cities to which the gospel came in that way.

Colosse was located in Asia Minor, between 100 and 125 miles due east of Ephesus in the region which the ancient world knew as Phrygia. When the Romans conquered this territory, they incorporated Phrygia into their province of Asia. Today it is part of Turkey. At the time of the Apostle Paul, Colosse formed a right triangle with two others cities, Hierapolis and Laodicea, both of which lay about eleven or twelve miles to the north and west.

These three cities, all of which are mentioned in Paul's epistle to the Colossians, were situated in the valley of the Lycus River, not far from the Lycus' junction with the rather well-known Meander River. Colosse was the oldest of the three sister cities. It was beautifully and strategically located, straddling the Lycus, with mountains to the north and south. The great eastern highway passed through Colosse on its way from Ephesus to the Euphrates River. As early as 480 B.C. ancient writers described Colosse as a "city inhabited, prosperous and great."

The Lycus Valley lies in an area frequently plagued by earthquakes and volcanic activity. Soon after the epistle to the Colossians was written, a great earthquake devastated the entire valley. But volcanic ground is also fertile ground. The rich meadows of the Lycus Valley proved ideal for raising sheep. Consequently, the clothing industry of the area flourished. In addition, the waters of the Lycus contained chalky deposits which were ideal for use in dyeing cloth. It is not surprising, therefore, that the cities in this valley prospered, although in the course of time their fortunes varied widely.

Despite the fact that Colosse was the oldest of the three cities in the valley, its fortunes had declined considerably by the time of the Apostle Paul. After the Romans took over the territory, Laodicea began to flourish as an industrial center. It became famous for the fine, black wool its sheep produced. Because of a change in the road system it became the junction where the eastern highway met four other roads. These and other factors eventually brought Laodicea the trade, commerce and prestige that once belonged to Colosse.

Hierapolis, too, had a special attraction. In volcanic regions there are many chasms out of which vapors and springs arise. These springs were thought by the ancients to have special healing powers. So Hierapolis became a famous spa. By the thousands people came to drink or bathe in its "healing" waters. Many of these springs and caves were dedicated to heathen deities.

So people who came to the Lycus Valley for health and pleasure came to Hierapolis. Those who were interested in trade or politics came to Laodicea. But already two generations before Paul wrote the epistle that bears its name, Colosse had deteriorated into a small, unimportant village that was in the process of decay. Even today the ruins of Laodicea and Hierapolis are quite impressive. The ruins of Colosse are barely noticeable. Yet to the church located in that unimportant and deteriorating city the Lord's Spirit, through the Apostle Paul, addressed a letter of lasting significance.

Paul himself may well have passed through Colosse on his third mission journey. But the fact that he says he has not met most of the Colossian Christians personally seems to indicate that he never stopped to do mission work there. The actual work in the city was done by a man named Epaphras, whom Paul praises in this epistle as a "dear fellow servant." Epaphras was probably one of those who first heard the gospel from Paul at Ephesus, then returned to his home town to begin a Christian congregation there, perhaps even under the apostle's direction. Although there was a large Jewish population in the Lycus Valley, the Christian congregation in Colosse consisted primarily of Gentile converts. Among the prominent members of the congregation were a man named Philemon and his family. Paul addressed a personal epistle to him. We will speak more of them in our study of that epistle, which is also included in this volume.

Four or five years after the Colossian congregation was founded, its pastor, Epaphras, came to Rome to visit the Apostle Paul. Paul, we recall, was a prisoner at the time, awaiting a hearing before the imperial court. You may wish to review this entire matter by considering once more the introduction to this volume. There was a definite, urgent reason that Epaphras made the 1300-mile journey, mostly by foot, to the imperial capital. Although he could report to Paul that the gospel had borne fruit in Colosse and in the entire region and that the fruits of faith and love were evident in the congregation, Epaphras was filled with anxious concern for the Christians he served. Their loyalty to Jesus and the gospel was being threatened by a new teaching.

On the surface, this teaching seemed to be quite similar to the gospel that Epaphras had learned from Paul. Like the apostle's gospel, this new teaching claimed to be a universal message suitable for Jew and Gentile alike. It, too, acknowledged that a gulf existed between man and God and taught a redemption that could bridge that gulf. It claimed to honor and worship Christ. Closely analyzed, however, this new teaching was an utter distortion of the gospel, a "deceptive philosophy" invented by men and shot through with false, human ideas.

Epaphras apparently sensed the problem, but he may have felt unqualified or inadequte to oppose it effectively. So he appealed to Paul, who was well schooled in the ways of both Greeks and Jews and had a unique ability to get to the heart of a problem. Paul was only too willing to help Epaphras in his battle for the gospel truth.

What was this false teaching about which Epaphras was so concerned and which prompted Paul to write this epistle? We shall discuss its various elements as we meet them in the epistle itself. It will be beneficial, however, for us to try to get a bit of an overview here of the so-called "Colossian heresy" as a background for our study of Colossians.

It is difficult for us to get a complete picture of the religious system being promoted by the false teachers in Colosse. Paul does not oppose their error by setting up his opponents' propositions or by refuting them point by point. Perhaps this was intentional. The apostle certainly did not intend to dignify false teaching by giving a full description of it. What is clear, however, is that the false doctrine being promoted in Colosse was a man-invented religion of self-redemption. It sought to combine both Jewish and pagan ideas with the Christian gospel to produce what its supporters boasted was a "more complete" gospel than Paul and Epaphras taught.

The Jewish element of the Colossian false teaching included a strong interest in Old Testament rituals, laws and ceremonies. From chapter 2 we learn that the false teachers attached a special significance to circumcision, dietary laws and the observance of Old Testament holidays. In fact, it appears as if they even went beyond the laws of Moses in their demand for self-denial and harsh treatment of the body.

These ideas were combined with a pagan, philosophical/superstitious interest in the spirit world and in the worship of angels. There was a hypocritical show of humility combined with an arrogant claim to having received special revelations. Over all of this seems to have hovered the idea that the Christianity that Paul and Epaphras taught was too simple and unsophisticated, too easy. A higher wisdom, the false teachers proclaimed, was necessary to achieve "complete Christianity." And they, of course, possessed that wisdom. They used code words like "fullness," "perfection" and "knowledge" to demean the apostles' teachings and promote their own.

The overall effect of this Colossian heresy was to entice people away from relying for salvation on the finished work of Christ. The false teachers wanted those who listened to them to accept instead of the simple gospel a human religious philosophical system that, for all intents and purposes, negated Jesus' ministry and emaciated his gospel.

What Epaphras sensed, and what the Apostle Paul clearly saw, was that this "new teaching" called into question, yes, totally denied the sufficiency of Christ. It denied the completeness of Christ's atonement, as well as Christ's power to furnish believers with the spiritual strength to live godly lives. What made it all the more dangerous was the fact that those who promoted this false teaching did not bill it as a substitute for the gospel, but as something that could supplement the gospel and help Christians reach "perfection," "fullness" and "complete salvation." Without *directly* denying the authority and power of Christ, the Colossian heresy promoted practices and teachings that cast a veil over his glory.

In his epistle to the Colossians Paul does not debate the false teachers. He simply overwhelms their errors by confronting the Colossians with the full riches of the gospel of Christ. Throughout the letter there is constant emphasis on the greatness of Christ. The apostle knows that the more thoroughly the Colossian believers understand the person and work of Christ, the better equipped they will be to recognize and reject errors like the one seeking to win its way into their congregation.

What Paul says about Christ in this epistle is not something new or something that is not found in his other epistles, but in this particular epistle he emphasizes in an especially powerful and persuasive way the divine teachings concerning the eternal Son of God. With clarity and forcefulness he shows the relevancy of Christ for the church and for individual believers for all time. Christ, he teaches, is the Creator and Sustainer of the universe, true God from all eternity together with the Father. And he is the Savior, the God-man, who by his blood has reconciled sinners to God. He is the Redeemer, Reconciler and Restorer of the sinful human race. He is and remains the real source of power for believers' lives of faith.

So in paragraph after powerful paragraph he exalts Christ as the all-sufficient Savior. Paul, with inspired insight, takes the very words the false teachers are using and throws them back against those teachers by filling them with Christ. Knowledge, fullness, perfection in the real sense, he shows, are all found only in Christ. It was not those who proclaimed the "simple" gospel, but those who boasted of their own philosophy and wisdom who were mired in the crude and elementary religious ideas of natural man who believes that he can and must do something to earn or help earn his salvation.

Christians don't need human philosophy and wisdom to be complete in their Christianity. They are already complete in Christ. In Christ alone, the very Christ the Colossians knew, and in the gospel they had received they could find perfect salvation and all the treasures of divine wisdom. Faithful Epaphras had preached that divinely given gospel in Colosse. To that gospel the Colossians needed to cling. They should not allow themselves to be intimidated by the claim of those who proposed a "more complete" or "superior" gospel.

Paul wrote his letter to the Colossians at about the same time he wrote letters to the Ephesians and to Philemon. He sent all three letters to their destinations with one of his co-workers, Tychicus. Tychicus was accompanied on his journey by Onesimus, the runaway slave who had become a Christian and whom Paul was now sending back to his master Philemon in Colosse. This fact may explain why the section on slave/master relationships is longer than the others that Paul outlines in Colossians 3:18 — 4:1. It may also be the reason why, throughout the epistle, Paul appears to give special emphasis to the virtue of forgiveness.

The message of Colossians is one of great practical value also for us twentieth-century Christians. We, too, live in an age that puts a high premium on knowledge and learning. In our day, as in the apostle's, human wisdom and learning are often allowed to sit in judgment on the Scriptures and on the gospel the Scriptures reveal. Today's so-called "higher criticism" resembles the Colossian heresy in its supposition that the "traditional" gospel is too simple and must be supplemented, or at the very least explained, by learned human scholars, if we are to know it in its "complete" form. A more sophisticated kind of Christianity, we are told, is necessary for our twentieth-century world.

As children of God we, of course, do not despise learning or exalt ignorance. But we cannot expect secular, human knowledge to solve the world's ills, because that knowledge does not address and cannot cure man's greatest problem, namely sin. Only Christ can solve this problem. Knowing and trusting in him remains the ultimate answer, the ultimate spiritual wisdom. The unbelieving scholar may sneer, but in Colossians the apostle reminds us again that in Christ are hid all the treasures of wisdom and knowledge.

The message of Colossians reinforces in us the precious truth that, whether we are educated in this world's wisdom or not, we Christians can rest assured that we have absolutely everything we need for time and for eternity in Christ. In our sophisticated, technological age, no less than in the apostle's age, Christ is all in all. We are complete in him.

The Colossian heresy was a heresy primarily because it reflected a defective view of Christ's person and work. If this false teaching had been allowed to continue unchecked, it would have starved the church of its vitality and undercut its witness. To combat that error aimed at Christianity's very heart, Paul in Colossians presents perhaps the most complete treatment of Christology, the doctrine of Christ, found anywhere in the New Testament. We who confess Jesus as "God of God, Light of light, very God of very God, begotten not made, being of one substance with the Father, by whom

109

all things were made," can return over and over again to the inspired verses of Colossians to reinforce our faith in and loyalty to that Christ, whose superior glory and complete sufficiency the apostle here sets forth so clearly and brilliantly.

From the time that this epistle was written to our own day the clear message of the gospel and salvation by grace through faith in Christ has been blurred and obscured by many false teachers. This includes the first century Judaizers, the monastics of the Middle Ages, and the modern day religious cults, all of whom would supplement the "simple" gospel with legalistic regulations and embellishments of human wisdom.

In Colossians Paul cuts through all the confusion of human laws and ideas and simply and directly points us to Christ. Christ is sufficient for our eternal salvation, and he is sufficient for our day-to-day living as his children. The message of this epistle speaks mightily to twentieth-century man, just as it did to first-century man. May it speak mightily to us as in this splendid epistle the apostle leads us again to see and to find our all in all in the all-sufficient Christ.

Outline of Colossians

Theme: Jesus, the All-Sufficient Savior

Greeting and Thanksgiving (1:1-14)
I. Jesus Is Sufficient for Our Faith (1:15-2:23)
    A. Jesus Is the Supreme Lord (1:15-23)
    B. The Gospel Ministry Proclaims the All-Sufficient Christ (1:24-2:5)
    C. The All-Sufficient Christ Gives Freedom from Human Regulations (2:6-23)
II. Jesus Is Sufficient for Our Christian Lives (3:1-4:6)
    A. The All-Sufficient Christ Gives Power for Holy Living (3:1-17)

B. The All-Sufficient Christ Sanctifies Our Family Relationships (3:18-4:1)
C. The All-Sufficient Christ Enables Us to Live Lives of Prayer and Wisdom (4:2-6)

Greetings and Conclusion (4:7-18)

GREETING AND THANKSGIVING
COLOSSIANS 1:1-14

Greeting

1 **Paul, an apostle of Christ Jesus by the will of God, and Timothy our brother, ²To the holy and faithful brothers in Christ at Colosse: Grace and peace to you from God our Father.**

Paul's greeting to the Colossians is similar to the greetings in his other epistles. The name of the author is mentioned first, then the person or persons addressed, followed by a formal word of greeting. In this epistle Paul formally introduced himself to the Colossians. He had never visited Colosse, and he had most likely never met most of the Christians there.

Nevertheless, he could write to them and they, together with believers of every generation to come, should receive his message with respect because of his calling. Paul was an apostle, an official spokesman for the Lord Jesus. He had received his apostolic office because the Lord himself had called him to it. He was writing to the Colossians in his official capacity as an apostle, an ambassador of the Lord. Through Paul the Lord himself was addressing the Colossians in this inspired epistle and still addresses us.

Timothy was in Rome with Paul when the apostle wrote this letter. Paul calls this faithful assistant "our brother." Paul, Timothy and the Colossians enjoyed a close, brotherly relationship, even if they had never personally met. By virtue of their common faith they belonged to the same spiritual family. Paul's epistle, though apostolic in its authority, is going to be brotherly in spirit.

The addressees of the letter are the "holy and faithful brothers in Christ at Colosse." "Holy ones" (saints) are those who have been set apart from the world by the Lord to serve and glorify him. The Colossian Christians and all who believe in Jesus are holy ones. The members of the congregation at Colosse had been faithful to the Lord Jesus until the time Paul wrote to them. The purpose of this letter was to encourage them in that faithfulness. Although it was to be shared with the believers in Laodicea, and eventually with every Christian congregation of the New Testament age, this epistle was specifically directed to the congregation at Colosse and to the struggles and troubles it faced.

With those two words that mean so much to every Christian Paul lovingly greets those whom he regards as brothers and sisters in Christ: "Grace and peace to you." Grace is God's unmerited love for sinners, love that he demonstrated in the redemptive work of Jesus. Peace is that peace of heart and conscience that results from the assurance God gives to believers that their sins are all forgiven and he is at peace with them. No greater blessings can be pronounced on anyone than the blessings of grace and peace. The apostle identifies God the Father as the giver of peace. God the Son is not mentioned, as he is in many of Paul's salutations. This is perhaps because in the body of the epistle Paul will launch into a detailed description of the Son and his sufficiency for believers.

Thanksgiving and Prayer

[3]We always thank God, the Father of our Lord Jesus Christ, when we pray for you, [4]because we have heard of your faith in Christ Jesus and of the love you have for all the saints — [5]the faith and love that spring from the hope that is stored up for you in heaven and that you have already heard about in the word of truth, the gospel [6]that has come to you. All over the world this

113

gospel is bearing fruit and growing, just as it has been doing among you since the day you heard it and understood God's grace in all its truth. ⁷You learned it from Epaphras, our dear fellow servant, who is a faithful minister of Christ on our behalf, ⁸and who also told us of your love in the Spirit.

Cultured writers in Paul's day often followed their greetings with a thanksgiving. Paul likewise offers a thanksgiving here. This thanksgiving, however, rises to a level far above that of any secular writer, because it is offered to the true God, the "Father of our Lord Jesus Christ." From eternity Jesus and the Father exist in that Father/Son relationship, and through the Son all spiritual blessings flow to believers from the Father.

When Paul wrote this epistle, there were grave dangers threatening the faith of the Colossians. These dangers stemmed from false teachings which downgraded the person and the work of Christ. Paul begins with this thankful affirmation of Christ's eternal relationship to the Father and its blessed consequences for believers, and throughout this epistle he makes countless tactful yet pertinent references to the spiritual dangers the Colossians are facing. He also encourages them to stand firm in Christ.

Before he begins with his specific warnings and encouragements in the body of his epistle, Paul gives thanks. He thanks God that the Colossians are believers. From all the reports that he has heard concerning them, the apostle is convinced of the sincerity of the Colossians' faith and love. He is especially thankful that they are continually giving evidence of their faith in loving concern for one another. Every believer ought constantly to have his fellow believer on his heart and seize every opportunity to give tangible evidence of that love. The Colossians were doing that within their congregational fellowship and their wider Christian fellowship. Would the apostle be able to commend us and our congregations with the same thankful joy?

The Colossians' faith and love, Paul says, sprang from hope. Christians' characteristics interact with one another. The more there is of one, the more there will be of another. That's the way it works with the well-known triad of faith, hope and love. Through God's gospel promises the Holy Spirit works in believers' hearts. As believers then patiently and confidently wait for God's promises to be fulfilled in the glory of eternity, their Spirit-instilled hope interacts mightily with faith and love, and they grow in all three.

The Colossians had received precious heavenly treasures through the message of the gospel, the word of truth that had been proclaimed to them. Paul was writing to them to encourage them to hold fast to that word of truth. Another word, claiming to be truth, was trying to gain entrance into their hearts, but neither that word nor any other word could compare with the greatness of the gospel.

The gospel the Colossians possessed was no mere "fly-by-night" message proclaimed by some secretive, local sect. It was a universal message of truth and life. The wonderful change that the gospel had brought about in the Colossians' hearts and lives was being duplicated in the hearts and lives of people all over the world. Its influence was being felt by ever increasing numbers of people as it made its way into region after region, producing fruit for Christ in people's hearts and lives.

The progress of the gospel in that first Christian century was nothing short of astounding. From just twelve apostles and perhaps several hundred other followers of Jesus at the time of the Ascension, historians estimate that by the time the last apostle (John) entered eternity the number of Christians had grown to half a million.

115

The Apostle Paul played a central role in that amazing story. We marvel at the superhuman efforts this one-time persecutor of Christians expended to carry the gospel into city after city and region after region. Even as a prisoner he was sharing the gospel with all in Rome with whom he came in contact.

But Paul makes no mention of himself or his labors here. Personal plaudits mattered little to him. He knew the credit all belonged to the gospel itself, the universal message through which God's power works in human hearts. Nor does the gospel's work cease in those hearts after it brings people to faith. It continues to work in the hearts of believers, and its power enables believers to bring forth faith's rich fruits. These fruits, too, were evident in Colosse and in the surrounding area.

Paul's implications in all that he says here are clear. The Colossians possessed the gospel, the word of truth. That gospel is universal, and it is sufficient. It needs no changes or improvements. It does not have to be supplemented by human wisdom. The Colossians would do well to treasure the gospel and not to listen to those who wanted to deprive them of the gospel. Twentieth-century believers would do well to do the same.

Epaphras was the Lord's servant who had first preached the gospel in Colosse. He was still the pastor of the Colossian congregation. It was Epaphras who had come to Rome to share his concern about the threat to the gospel that was confronting the congregation and to seek Paul's advice and help. Paul calls Epaphras "our dear fellow servant, who is a faithful minister of Christ on our behalf." Paul was grateful for the diligent work Epaphras had done in Colosse. Since he himself was not able to personally bring the gospel there, he considered the work Epaphras did to be work "on his behalf." He felt personally indebted to Epaphras for doing that work. We ought to feel the same kind of personal gratitude to the missionaries and nurses who take the gospel into other lands in our place, as our representatives.

By his favorable description of Epaphras Paul puts his apostolic stamp of approval on the Colossian pastor's work. The gospel that Epaphras preached in Colosse was the very same gospel that Paul and Timothy preached. Even more important, it was Christ's gospel. Any message that claimed to be gospel, but did not agree with the gospel Epaphras taught, was neither Paul's message nor Christ's.

⁹For this reason, since the day we heard about you, we have not stopped praying for you and asking God to fill you with the knowledge of his will through all spiritual wisdom and understanding. ¹⁰And we pray this in order that you may live a life worthy of the Lord and may please him in every way: bearing fruit in every good work, growing in the knowledge of God, ¹¹being strengthened with all power according to his glorious might so that you may have great endurance and patience, and joyfully ¹²giving thanks to the Father, who has qualified you to share in the inheritance of the saints in the kingdom of light. ¹³For he has rescued us from the dominion of darkness and brought us into the kingdom of the Son he loves, ¹⁴in whom we have redemption, the forgiveness of sins.

Paul was a firm believer in prayer. Here he assures the Colossian Christians that he has been praying for them. Prayer for all the Christian congregations was a part of his daily routine. From the time they had first heard about the congregation in Colosse, Paul says, he, Timothy and the others had remembered the Colossian believers in their prayers. Encouraged by the blessings God had already bestowed on those believers, Paul and his co-workers constantly asked for more. Knowing that the apostle and his fellow workers were praying for them should have made the Colossians even more receptive to the encouragements and warnings Paul was about to give them in this epistle.

The specific requests that Paul made in his prayers for the Colossians were dictated by their special needs. Reading between the lines of Paul's prayer requests, we see some rather direct references to the situation in Colosse. The apostle's first and basic request for the Colossians was that the Lord would fill them with a clear knowledge of his will.

Paul wanted the Colossians to have not just a fact knowledge, but a clear and penetrating insight, a heart-transforming and life-renewing knowledge of God's revelation in Christ. This knowledge, for which every Christian ought to pray, is both satisfying and practical. It includes wisdom, the ability to properly apply one's faith in various situations, as well as understanding, the ability to evaluate spiritual matters and reject that which is false and cling to that which is true.

The opponents of the gospel in Colosse boasted a great deal about their knowledge. Clear knowledge of God's word and will, Paul says, will enable the Colossians to see through all false claims and remain faithful to the Lord. Paul's prayer surely also included the request that God would use the very words he was writing to the Colossians to strengthen their knowledge and their hold on the truth.

Clear knowledge of God and his will guides the believer in conduct worthy of the Lord. Paul prays that the Colossians will conduct themselves in harmony with their believing relationship to the Lord. A Christian constantly and earnestly strives to please God by living a life in harmony with God's will. The more thoroughly God's children come to know him, the more they will mature in their faith-relationship with him, and the more they will desire to obey him by thinking, saying and doing those things that will be pleasing to the Lord whose name they bear.

With four phrases Paul describes in verses 10 and 11 the kind of Christian lives that he prays will characterize the Colossians. He prays that they will *bear fruit in every good work*. Good works, the thoughts, words and deeds that please God, are the fruits of faith. As Christians grow in their knowledge of God and his love, their faith grows. A growing faith will reveal itself more and more in the fruits of practical holiness.

By mentioning *growing in knowledge* as an element in a God-pleasing life, Paul shows how a Christian life can be seen as a perfect circle. Knowledge of God and his saving will for sinners is the basic blessing. It, in turn, results in love for God and in the desire to serve God with a holy life. An important element in a life that pleases God is using God's means of grace, the gospel in word and sacrament. As Christians use the means of grace, the Holy Spirit works in their hearts to strengthen them in faith and in the knowledge of God and his will, especially his saving will for them. Thus Christians come full circle.

In spiritual things, as in many other things, knowledge is *power*. As Christians come to know their Lord more deeply, he fills them with the spiritual strength that enables them to confess, "I can do everything through him, who gives me strength." Through the gospel the Holy Spirit fills believers with his strength, not in a measured or sparing way, but in proportion to his limitless power. That strength enables believers to perform their tasks and live their Christian lives confidently and without fear. It gives them the courage to endure hardships, persecutions and temptations with brave patience and even to forgive those who oppress them.

Finally, a God-pleasing life is marked by *joyful thanksgiving*. Paul's entire epistle to the Philippians is an encouragement to joy and thanksgiving, even in time of tribulation. He repeats that encouragement here.

119

As he brings this extraordinary prayer to a close, Paul highlights once more the most important reason Christians have for giving thanks. God the Father, to whom believers' thanks should ever ascend, has "qualified you to share in the inheritance of the saints in the kingdom of light." In the Old Testament the Lord provided the people of Israel with an inheritance in the land of Canaan. New Testament believers share in an even better inheritance, a spiritual one.

The Colossian believers, who had mainly been drawn from the Gentile world, had at one time been strangers to God. They had been alienated from the church, God's kingdom. Since Adam's fall into sin all human beings, Jews and Gentiles alike are by the very nature that they inherit from their sinful parents, enemies of God and strangers to his kingdom. But by his grace God had qualified the Colossians to share in the inheritance of his saints in light. This was something God did and not something they deserved or worked for. An inheritance is a gift, something not earned but freely given. Furthermore, their spiritual inheritance is not something for which believers are naturally fit, but something for which they have been "qualified" by God.

The great inheritance of which Paul speaks is called the "inheritance of the saints in light." "Saints," separated ones, is simply another name for believers. "Light" in Scripture means all of the things that have to do with God and holiness, spiritual wisdom, salvation and life. In his undeserved love for sinners God qualifies them to share in his kingdom of light. He reaches out through the gospel to rescue them from the kingdom of darkness and death and brings them into the kingdom of Jesus, his Son.

Ancient peoples who were conquered by other nations were often transplanted from their homeland, where they were free, to unfamiliar foreign lands, where they were slaves. In believers' spiritual lives, however, God has graciously done just the opposite. He has transplanted sinners like the Colossians and the apostle (notice how Paul in a surge of emotion changes the "you" of verse 12 to "us" in verse 13), as well as us twentieth-century Christians, from the spiritual kingdom of darkness, ignorance and death to the kingdom of wisdom, life and light in Jesus, the Savior.

God did this for sinful human beings by one mighty act of love in human history. In the fullness of time he sent his Son whom he loves into our world of sin and shame. That Son, though he was and remained true God, took on a true human nature and became the substitute for the whole human race. He lived a perfect life to satisfy God's law in man's place and to gain for sinners a righteousness that none have by nature. On Calvary's cross he shed his blood and died to pay the penalty God's perfect justice demanded for man's numberless transgressions of his law. The Father accepted his Son's work on man's behalf. By raising Jesus from the dead he declared that the world's sin had all been paid for. Thus he qualified a world of sinners for the eternal inheritance and rescued them from Satan's kingdom.

Individual sinners personally receive these blessings when the Holy Spirit through the gospel brings them the news of God's perfect salvation in Christ Jesus, then works in their hearts by that same gospel the faith that believes the message and trusts in Jesus. The whole world of sinners has been justified in Christ Jesus; that is the central teaching of Scripture. And the primary purpose of Scripture is to bring individual sinners to faith in Christ, so that they share in his perfect righteousness and inherit eternal life. If these truths are lost, there is no Christian faith left, and there is no salvation. Paul wanted the Colossians to remember and continually thank God for these saving truths.

Each of us, too, will want to be continually thanking the Lord for the blessings of his grace in our lives. Daily and earnestly we need to seek his help to grow through his word in clear knowledge of him, a knowledge that will be a living force throughout every area of our lives. Just hearing or reading this magnificent thanksgiving and prayer should have lifted the Colossians' spirits and made them eager to hear the rest of what Paul had to say to them.

Paul's words still provide Christians with a wonderful model for the thanksgivings and prayers we ought always to be raising to God, both for ourselves and for our fellow believers. Reading this thanksgiving and prayer and applying it to ourselves ought to lift our spirits, too, and make us eager to drink in the spiritual nourishment that the apostle will provide for us in the rest of this important epistle.

JESUS IS SUFFICIENT FOR OUR FAITH
COLOSSIANS 1:15 — 2:23

Jesus Is the Supreme Lord

[15]He is the image of the invisible God, the firstborn over all creation. [16]For by him all things were created: things in heaven and on earth, visible and invisible, whether thrones or powers or rulers or authorities; all things were created by him and for him. [17]He is before all things, and in him all things hold together. [18]And he is the head of the body, the church; he is the beginning and the firstborn from among the dead, so that in everything he might have the supremacy. [19]For God was pleased to have all his fullness dwell in him, [20]and through him to reconcile to himself all things, whether things on earth or things in heaven, by making peace through his blood, shed on the cross.

[21]Once you were alienated from God and were enemies in your minds because of your evil behavior. [22]But now he has reconciled you by Christ's physical body through death to present you holy in his sight, without blemish and free from accusation — [23]if you continue in your faith, established and firm, not moved from the hope held out in the gospel. This is the gospel that you heard and that has been proclaimed to every creature under heaven, and of which I, Paul, have become a servant.

The Apostle Paul now launches into the main theme of his letter, the supremacy and unique greatness of Jesus Christ. Paul felt a need to write to the Colossians about this subject because the false teachers who were trying to gain entrance into their congregation were promoting teachings that robbed Christ of the glory and honor due him. It is difficult for us to get a clear and complete picture of this false teaching that was troubling the Colossians. Paul never mentions its exact features directly or refutes the errorists point by point (see also the comments on this matter in the introduction to this epistle).

The false teachers may have given lip service to Jesus and claimed to believe in him as the Savior, but it is clear that they also regarded other things and other powers as having saving value. They were teaching that the simple gospel was not enough to save sinners, but had to be supplemented with their teachings and ideas. But such teachings robbed Jesus of his glory as the only and all-sufficient Savior, the eternal Son of God and only Redeemer of mankind.

Paul's answer to this "Colossian heresy" is a stirring and positive presentation of the exalted nature of Christ and his complete sufficiency for all of mankind's needs. As one writer put it, Paul does not try to argue with the false teachers; he overwhelms them by confronting them with the true gospel of Christ.

In the first five verses of this section we have another of those sublime passages of the New Testament that seem to jump right off the printed page. It's a literary gem, an inspired, hymnlike confession of the supremacy and greatness of Christ. This section contains several words and expressions we don't find anywhere else in Paul's writings. This is possibly because Paul was here taking some of the terms the enemies of the gospel were arrogantly using in connection with their false teaching, emptying them of their wrong meaning and filling them up again with real significance by connecting them with Christ.

Because Paul here describes in human terms the greatness of Christ which passes human understanding, we may have trouble grasping the full meaning of what the Holy Spirit through the apostle is telling us. This is one of those sections of Scripture that must be read, digested and read again. But that is something that we shall willingly do, because the apostle provides us here with a magnificent testimony to the person and the work of our Lord Jesus. This is a confession of faith that ought to strengthen us in our faith in the all-sufficient Christ. This clear confession can help us to reject any teaching that fails to give Christ the glory he deserves.

In verses 15-17 Paul describes Christ's unique greatness in his relationship to the world of creation. Throughout this epistle Paul simply takes it for granted that the Lord Jesus, whom the Colossians have received in faith, is truly God. He feels no need to argue the point. Paul has personally seen the exalted Christ, when Jesus revealed himself to him as God on the road to Damascus. So, whenever Paul speaks of Jesus or describes him, he describes him as the eternal Son of the eternal Father, in no way inferior to the Father and possessing all the Father's divine characteristics.

The apostle begins his description of Christ's unique greatness in these verses by referring to him first as the "image of the invisible God." The word "image" here means more than just likeness. Jesus is more than "like God." Jesus is God. He is the perfect expression, the very personification of God.

The Scriptures teach us that the first man and the first woman were created in the "image of God" and that now through the Spirit believers are "renewed in the image of God." The image of God in man is something created by God and derived from him. It is a reflection of God's glory and holiness.

Christ, however, was not "created in the image of God." That image was an essential part of his very being from all eternity. "I am in the Father and the Father is in me," he tells us in John 14:10. In that same Gospel (John 10:30) he declares, "I and the Father are one." The writer to the Hebrews testifies concerning Jesus, "The Son is the radiance

125

of God's glory and the exact representation of his being" (Hebrews 1:3). Jesus is the "image of the invisible God" because HE IS GOD!

If the Son is the image of the invisible God, who is from everlasting to everlasting, the Son, too is from everlasting to everlasting. He is far above all created beings, above time and space, above all things. What Paul expresses here is what we confess in the Nicene Creed, that Jesus Christ is "God of God, Light of light, very God of very God, begotten, not made, being of one substance with the Father, by whom all things were made."

As the image of the invisible God, Jesus is also the perfect revelation of God to us. Jesus is God revealed to us for our salvation. No human being has ever seen God in his unveiled splendor. His nature as a spirit places him beyond the sight of men. If he were visible, sinners could not look at him without being destroyed by the consuming fire of his holiness.

In 1 Timothy 4:15, 16 Paul describes God as the "King of kings and Lord of lords, who alone is immortal and who lives in unapproachable light, whom no one has seen or can see." But in Jesus, his eternal Son, the invisible God has graciously made himself known to the world. Jesus took on a human nature like our own and came down to earth to make the Father known to men. He came to reveal the Father, especially in his love and grace.

The Apostle John, one of those who were privileged to walk and talk with Jesus while he was here on earth, wrote by inspiration: "No one has ever seen God, but God the One and Only, who is at the Father's side, has made him known" (John 1:18). Jesus told his disciples, "Anyone who has seen me has seen the Father" (John 14:9). In Jesus sinful human beings come to see and know the invisible, unapproachable God. Indeed, all who would know God must come to know him through Jesus Christ.

Moving to Christ's relationship to the created world, Paul describes him in verse 15 as "the firstborn over all creation." This title does not mean that Jesus is a created being. The title is not "first-created" but "first-born." There is a vast difference. The very next part of the verse tells us that Jesus is the Creator. What "firstborn" does mean is that Jesus is superior to every created being. He is before all creatures in time, because he is eternal, and he is above all in rank. The false teachers troubling the Colossians made much of ranks of spiritual beings, like angels. Jesus, Paul says, is above them all.

The unique greatness of Jesus in the created world is also evident in his work. He is not only the image of God, who existed before creation. He himself is the Creator of all things. All things in heaven were created by his power. So were all things on earth, both living and non-living things, with man as their glory and crown.

Even the invisible world, which those false teachers found so fascinating and about whose "ranks" (thrones, powers, rulers, authorities) they spent so much time speculating, were created by Christ. The false teachers apparently ascribed to angels and other spiritual beings a power independent of Christ. They encouraged Christians to worship them (see 2:18), but Paul here reaffirms the truth that Christ is the Creator also of all the creatures in the spirit world. Because he is their Creator, they are subject to him. The good angels are dedicated to his service. The fallen angels live in terror of him. Their power cannot even begin to match the power of Christ, their Creator.

But isn't God the Father the Creator of the world? we ask. It is true that Scripture ascribes the work of creation primarily to the Father. But in their activities that affect our world, all three persons of the Holy Trinity are always inseparably involved. Scripture pictures the Son and the Spirit as active in the creation of the world together with the Father. John's Gospel (John 1:1-3) tells us that Jesus was together with the Father at the creation of the world. In fact, as the divine Word Jesus was the agent of creation, the one who caused everything to come into being. "Through him all things were made; without him nothing was made that has been made." Christ is the Creator of all things, and all things were created for him. All creation exists for his praise. All things reflect his power and glory, and all things and all people are obligated to show his praises.

Christ created all things, and he continues to preserve them. There is a continuing interaction between Christ and the entire universe. In him all things hold together. The unity and order in the universe and the laws of nature are the expressions of Christ's will and power. If it were not for that power, everything in the universe would fly apart and be thrown into chaos, but in Christ they all wonderfully cohere.

The heathen philosophers of Paul's day, from whom the enemies of the gospel in Colosse had borrowed many of their "progressive" ideas, talked about a "living force" that holds everything in the universe together. Paul wants his readers to remember that what holds the world together is no vague, unidentifiable force. It is Jesus Christ. "In him we live and move and have our being," the apostle told the educated Greeks at Athens. Jesus is Lord of the universe.

The supremacy of Christ which extends over the whole created universe also extends, in a special way, over his church. He is the head of the body, the church, Paul says. The picture of the church as a body, with many interrelated members carrying out their various functions, is a familiar one to the readers of Paul's epistles, but the apostle's emphasis here is slightly different from that in the other references. In Romans and Ephesians Paul's lesson is that believers are members of the same body and must function harmoniously together for the sake of the church's well-being. Here the lesson is that the body has a wonderful head that rules and controls its every function. That head is Christ.

As a body cannot live without a head, the church cannot exist without Christ. The human head holds the brain, the nerve center of the body. Modern science has also discovered that the growth of the body is controlled from the head, by a tiny gland located at the base of the brain. Similarly, Christ is the church's organic head. It is only through him that the church can live and grow. And Christ is the church's ruling head. He exercises authority over the church, directs its every function and governs all things in the universe in the church's interest. On Christ alone the church depends for everything.

The church and all believers are dependent for their very existence on Christ. This is emphasized by the phrase, "He is the beginning." In Revelation 21:6 Jesus describes himself as the "Beginning and the End," the eternal one on whom his believers depend. By faith in him believers are sharers in all the blessings that belong to him as the eternal Son of God. "Firstborn from the dead" is a title that reminds us of the importance of his resurrection for our salvation. Jesus' resurrection guarantees that believers, too, will one day rise at his command. He holds the keys of death and the grave and has power over life and death. His resurrection, following his humiliation and death as the sinners' substitute, is the reaffirmation of his supremacy over all things.

With one majestic statement after another the apostle has risen higher and higher in his praise of the exalted Christ and his assertion of Christ's unique greatness. Christ is supreme before all the created world; he is supreme over his redeemed congregation; he is supreme in the resurrection and the glory of the life to come. Now he brings all those greatnesses together into one grand statement, "For God was pleased to have all his fullness dwell in him." We shall discuss more about the term "fullness" in our study of chapter 2:9.

Was "fullness" another of those words the false teachers used in such an arrogant way? Perhaps it was. But in the face of all the claims about fullness the apostle triumphantly asserts here that real and absolute fullness, fullness in its greatest sense, can be found only in Christ. In him all the fullness of God's grace and glory reside. Through him all the fullness of the divine thoughts and counsels is expressed. He possesses all fullness from eternity, and there is no domain in time in which he is not supreme.

The fact that all divine fullness rests in Christ is a rich source of blessing for believers. For in Christ and through the divine fullness he possesses, God was pleased to bring about a reconciliation between himself and the world of sinful human beings. By nature, since Adam's fall, sinners are alienated from God and the objects of his wrath. But God's thoughts toward fallen humanity are thoughts of peace and not of evil. Through Christ, the Son of his love, God has taken the initiative and brought about peace between sinners and himself.

The Son of God in whom all fullness resides, came into this world of sin, not to vaunt his glory, but to humble himself and to shed his blood on Calvary's cross. He came to take the curse of man's sin on himself and to pay for its guilt, so that the broken relationship between sinners and God might be repaired and changed from a relationship of warfare and enmity to one of blessedness and peace. The gospel's opponents in Colosse spoke much about making peace with God and removing the barriers which separate God and man by building ladders to God with their own rituals and schemes and works and deeds. Paul brushes all this away as irrelevant and unnecessary. Jesus has already done all that is necessary to remove the barriers that sin created between God and man. He has done all this by his cross and the shedding of his blood. Through them our guilt is pardoned and his righteousness is credited to us. He earned full forgiveness for all sinners.

Individual sinners receive that forgiveness as their very own by faith. The reconciliation that Jesus brought about is perfect and complete, including the whole created world. When man fell into sin, the whole created world was affected by the consequences of sin. What had been a beautiful and perfect world became a very imperfect world. Christ's redemptive work, however, re-established peace between the sinful world and the holy God.

Human beings receive the blessings of that peace spiritually by faith already here in time. In eternity they will experience them perfectly and permanently. In the resurrection world even the created world that was corrupted by man's sin will be restored to perfection again. We do not understand all the details of what that resurrection world will be like, but we do know that everything about it, including our own relationship to our Lord, will testify to the complete and perfect redemption and reconciliation accomplished by the all-sufficient Christ.

Paul wanted the Colossians to be personally aware of Christ's supremacy in the realm of their salvation. They had been recipients of the spiritual blessings brought about by God's reconciliation of the world to himself. From their origin as sinners born of sinners, they had been alienated from God. They were strangers, shut out from God's mercy and love. They were enemies of God in their affections and dispositions, and their wicked actions revealed their inner hatred of God and their unwillingness to serve him.

But now, by a miracle of God's mercy, those same people had entered a new and wonderful relationship with God.

They had been made personal sharers in the reconciliation Jesus brought about between sinners and God. Because Jesus came into this world, took on a human nature and became man's substitute, because in his physical body Jesus bore the curse of sin and satisfied the justice of God, the Colossians' debt of sin, too, had been paid.

Through the gospel the Holy Spirit had entered their hearts to fill them with the faith by which they believed in Jesus and received his redemptive blessings as their very own. With Christ's righteousness and his redemptive payment for their sins credited to them, they could now stand without blemish and free from accusation before God. Jesus is supreme in the realm of salvation, and Jesus and his salvation are all-sufficient for believers' personal reconciliation with God.

It is only through the gospel that Christ and his redemptive blessings come to believers' lives and they share in the blessings of reconciliation, and it is only through the gospel that those who have been brought into that vital faith-relationship with Jesus are maintained and strengthened in their faith. The false teachers in Colosse were urging the Colossian believers to accept in place of the gospel a human message that claimed to be gospel, but was not gospel at all.

Firmness and a proper sense of purpose and direction were necessary. "Continue in the faith," Paul unashamedly urges. Don't let anyone move you from the gospel hope you have in Christ. Don't let any false teaching from without or sinful prompting from within cause you to turn away from the one message which joins you to Christ. Use all the spiritual energy the Holy Spirit has given you in Christ to flee from the false and cling to the true. Unfailingly renew your spiritual strength by returning again and again to the strength-giving and strength-maintaining gospel. Through the gospel maintain your hold on your all-sufficient Savior.

The pseudo-gospel that the false teachers were proclaiming in and around Colosse was a message with many strange elements peculiar to that rather small group of teachers, but the gospel Paul proclaimed was a universal message. It had been enthusiastically carried by the apostles and their successors into almost every part of the Roman world.

Human beings do not have to seek new and mystical ways to find Christ and his salvation. Human wisdom and philosophy are not necessary to discover him. All that sinners need to find Christ is the clear and simple message of the apostolic gospel. In the gospel the Colossians possessed Christ in all his fullness. No other revelations were necessary for them, nor are they for us.

The truths Paul has discussed in this lengthy section are primarily doctrinal. They express objective truths concerning Christ and the gospel. But they are also practical, perhaps more so than we might at first realize. Think of what the great truths Paul has so forcefully emphasized here mean for our lives. Jesus is supreme in the world of creation. He created all things, and he governs all things and holds them together with his almighty power. This assures us that, contrary to what we may sometimes think, the world is not in chaos. It is continually under the rule of our all-sufficient Lord and Savior. There is a plan, a divine purpose, in all that happens in our world and in our lives, a purpose determined and brought to pass by the Savior who loves us.

Sin, the world, the devil are not in control of this world. Jesus is. He sets limits to their wicked activities. Nothing in this world, no communistic menace, no bomb or economic depression or accident; nothing in our lives, including the worst imaginable tragedies, can separate us from our Savior or from the hands of love in which he continually holds us. Day after day he is moving this world forward to the end of the age, when he, by his almighty power, will deliver us completely and forever from the effects and consequences of sin, bring an end to this present evil world, and make all things wonderfully new in the eternal glory that he has promised to share with us, his children by faith.

There is blessed assurance, too, in the truth that Jesus is supreme in the world of salvation. The gospel sets before us the great truth that in Christ and his redemptive work our salvation is complete. We do not have to add one single thing. Once in history the eternal Son of God gave his life to provide a reconciliation between sinners and God. The blessings of that reconciliation are personally ours by faith, which is also his free gift to us through the gospel. The gospel reveals to us and connects us with the all-sufficient Christ.

Today there are many who, like the false teachers at Colosse, belittle the gospel and regard it as something irrelevant for our modern age. Their logic is alluring and their words are enticing, especially to our sinful natures, as they urge us to give up the gospel. But if we truly appreciate the unique greatness of our Savior and if we understand that it is only through the gospel that we are joined to the Savior and his blessings, any idea of giving that gospel up or exchanging it for something "better" will quickly be rejected. Continue! Paul says, Stand firm! Hold fast to the all-sufficient Christ and the gospel that proclaims him. To Paul's encouragement we add a loud Amen.

The Gospel Ministry Proclaims the All-Sufficient Christ

24Now I rejoice in what was suffered for you, and I fill up in my flesh what is still lacking in regard to Christ's afflictions, for the sake of his body, which is the church. 25I have become its servant by the commission God gave me to present to you the word of God in its fullness — 26the mystery that has been kept hidden for ages and generations, but is now disclosed to the saints. 27To them

God has chosen to make known among the Gentiles the glorious riches of this mystery, which is Christ in you, the hope of glory. [28]We proclaim him, admonishing and teaching everyone with all wisdom, so that we may present everyone perfect in Christ. [29]To this end I labor, struggling with all his energy, which so powerfully works in me.

2 I want you to know how much I am struggling for you and for those at Laodicea, and for all who have not met me personally. [2]My purpose is that they may be encouraged in heart and united in love, so that they may have the full riches of complete understanding, in order that they may know the mystery of God, namely, Christ, [3]in whom are hidden all the treasures of wisdom and knowledge. [4]I tell you this so that no one may deceive you by fine-sounding arguments. [5]For though I am absent from you in body, I am present with you in spirit and delight to see how orderly you are and how firm your faith in Christ is.

The gospel to which the Colossians needed to hold fast was the universal gospel message of the all-sufficient Christ. Paul was a minister, a servant of that gospel. At the time he wrote this epistle, however, he was not making mission journeys or ministering to the Colossians in person as he desired to do. He was a political prisoner in Rome. He had been deprived of his freedom and was now suffering hardship for the sake of his faithful proclamation of the gospel.

The physical circumstances of the apostle's imprisonment may not have been particularly harsh, but the fact remained that Paul was not a free man. He could not move about and carry out his apostolic labors as he had in the past. For the apostle just that fact meant hardship and suffering. Instead of complaining about his situation, however, he rejoiced. He rejoiced because he knew that the troubles he was enduring confirmed his apostleship. He rejoiced because, as a servant of the gospel, he was more than willing to endure hardship on account of his work for Christ and on behalf of Christ's church.

As he suffered because of his commitment to Christ, Paul was filling up in his flesh what was still lacking in regard to Christ's afflictions for the sake of his body, the church. What does Paul mean with this unusual phrase? He cannot be saying that his sufferings, or the sufferings of any believer, completed Christ's redemptive sacrifice. Jesus' sufferings to atone for the world's sins were complete when from the cross he declared, "It is finished." His atoning sacrifice provided a full and perfect ransom payment for the sins of all the world. Paul consistently testifies to the all-sufficiency of Christ's atonement. So do the other sacred writers.

The expression "filling up what is lacking in Christ's afflictions" here is simply a reference to the treatment believers can expect as followers of Jesus in the world. When Jesus was here on earth, his enemies hated him. That hatred led them to reject him, falsely accuse him and finally even put him to death. Even after they crucified Jesus, his enemies were not satisfied. They are not satisfied yet. They want to continue to add to his afflictions. Since Jesus is no longer physically present on earth, the hatred that his enemies once directed toward him personally is now directed toward his disciples. By suffering for the sake of the gospel, therefore, Paul was undergoing hardship in Jesus' place. He was not doing it at all by himself, of course, but he was contributing his share, just as other believers were contributing theirs, to that measure of suffering the Lord has allotted to his believers on earth.

In his divine wisdom the Lord allows much suffering to come on certain believers for the gospel's sake. Paul and the other apostles certainly fell into that category. Other believers may not be called on to suffer much at all, but whenever believers suffer anything for the sake of their commitment to Christ, Jesus' afflictions are overflowing to them, and they are filling up what is still lacking in the afflictions of Christ.

Believers should not be surprised when they are called on to do this. The disciple is not above his master, and Jesus warned his followers that they could expect the hatred of a world that hated him. Fellowship, partnership with Jesus, means also sharing in his sufferings. Believers can still regard the mockery, ridicule and all the other physical and psychological blows struck against them because they are Christians as blows struck against Jesus himself.

Paul's sufferings as an apostle could also bring him calm joy, because he knew those sufferings were benefiting the church. When the enemies of the gospel directed a special measure of hatred and violence against well-known leaders of the church like Paul, the practical result was often that lesser-known Christians were spared. By enduring hardship as their apostle, Paul was deflecting from them some of the things the Colossians and others might otherwise have had to suffer. By his calm endurance and clear testimony even in suffering Paul was encouraging believers everywhere to follow his example and stand firm in the faith.

Paul's office as an apostle connected him in a special way with the Gentile church. He had been called and commissioned as an apostle to serve non-Jews like the Colossians. As their apostle he was now warning and encouraging those Gentile believers who were in danger of being misled by false teachers. Paul regarded his ministry as a service and himself as a servant entrusted with great riches, because he served a great master.

In Paul's day it was customary that certain servants of wealthy masters were appointed as stewards, or managers, and placed in charge of their master's entire estate. These servants had the right and the duty to dispense the master's wealth as necessary for the benefit of those in the household. The Apostle Paul had been commissioned by God as his manager, the servant who was to dispense God's spiritual treasures through the preaching of the gospel, especially to the Gentiles. He regarded that calling as a marvelous bless-ing of God's grace to him. Early in his life Paul (then known as Saul) had been a blasphemer of Christ and a persecutor of the church. But by a miracle of his grace (see Acts 9) God called Saul/Paul to be a follower of Christ and his servant in the ministry.

Paul never forgot that grace and that calling. Nor did he forget the great purpose of his ministry: to proclaim the word of God in all its fullness wherever God would send him. In carrying out his ministry Paul had proclaimed the gospel in a great circle from Jerusalem to Rome. Through his pupil Epaphras the Colossians had the spiritual riches of the gospel proclaimed to them.

At the heart of the message that Paul had been called to proclaim was "the mystery that has been kept hidden for ages and generations, but is now disclosed to the saints." The word "mystery" does not have to do with secrets or ceremonies known only to some exclusive group, as the false teachers apparently used the term. "Mystery" here means a truth that can be known only when God reveals it to men.

The great truths of forgiveness and salvation in Christ are a mystery to sinful human beings. In their naturally sinful, spiritually ignorant state, human beings cannot discover this mystery for themselves, but the mystery is made known as God discloses his will to men through the proclamation of the gospel.

In Old Testament times this mystery was revealed primar-ily to the people of Israel, but even they did not have the mystery made known in all its completeness. They were saved by faith in the coming Savior. How the Savior would carry out his work and break down the Old Testament barrier between the Jews and the Gentiles would not be fully revealed until Christ's appearance in the flesh.

In the New Testament age that mystery is fully revealed. Christ came to fulfill all the promises of God and to complete the work of salvation also for Gentiles. To his New Testament church that Savior has given the task of proclaiming the good news of salvation in all the world. The ascended Lord wants sinners everywhere to know him as their Savior. He wants them to hear the good news of "Christ in you, the hope of glory." The gospel announces to sinners that the hope for eternal glory lies in Christ Jesus alone, not in becoming Jewish or in following human regulations.

When sinners through the gospel come to faith in Jesus, he dwells in their hearts and transforms their lives. The fact that Jesus dwells in believers now is the basis for their hope. Yes, it is the guarantee that one day they will share in eternal glory with him. Christ is the heart of the gospel, the key which unlocks the mystery, the sinner's only hope for eternal glory. The gospel proclaims Christ and offers the blessings he earned for sinners, not just to one ethnic group or to an exclusive sect somewhere, but to all sinners everywhere.

To the Colossians, as well as to many others, Paul and his associates were proclaiming Christ. This was not just Paul's calling, it was his life. Even in his imprisonment he made use of every opportunity, both in person and by his letters, to make known far and wide the riches that believers possess in Christ. Paul's proclamation of Christ took the form of both counseling and teaching. To counsel means to warn and encourage. As he preached Christ, Paul actually pleaded with people to be reconciled to God. He presented the gospel in a warm and affectionate way, with an obvious personal concern for individual souls.

With that same deep emotion he warned against false teaching and error. The apostle's teaching was centered in Christ. His great aim was to hold Christ before his listeners and readers and to fill their hearts and lives with Christ. As the Lord's apostle he carried out all of this counseling and teaching in a wise, open and practical way. This was in sharp contrast to the devious and underhanded methods of his opponents.

Paul preached Christ with the great aim of bringing immortal souls to know and believe in Jesus and be saved. Nor did he neglect the spiritual growth of those who had already been brought to faith. He wanted to "present everyone perfect in Christ." Christians are still sinners. They will not reach perfection in their faith and lives here on earth, so they need to press on and strive constantly to grow toward full maturity in Christ. They need to work to maintain their faith and to grow in their Christian living. To help them achieve this growing and maturing, believers need constant, thorough instruction in God's word. In his ministry Paul provided such instruction.

Providing such encouragement and instruction from God's word to help believers grow and mature in faith and Christian living is also an essential task of the ministry today. Soul winning must be followed up by soul nourishing and soul conservation. If this is not done or if believers themselves do not regularly use the opportunities the church provides for them to hear and study God's word, their faith will deteriorate and may finally die altogether.

As an instrument in the Lord's hands to rescue souls from hell and to help them grow toward spiritual maturity, Paul eagerly threw himself into the work of his ministry. Constrained by the love of Christ and aware of the dangers threatening the faith of the Colossians and other believers, Paul toiled and labored in his ministry to the point of weariness and exhaustion. Like an athlete straining his entire being in a contest, Paul exerted himself to the limits of his physical strength to fulfill his ministry. He worked, he prayed and studied, he planned, he counseled, he wrote, he preached and taught, he bore witness with his life, he endured affliction.

How could one man accomplish so much? Paul says that as he struggled, the strength and energy that Christ gave him worked powerfully within him. From the Lord who had called him into the ministry Paul received the strength to carry out his ministry. In the Lord's strength Paul would leave no stone unturned, no effort unexpended, no battle unfought to win immortal souls for Christ and to help those who were already believers grow and mature in faith. Day after day, moment by moment the Spirit was at work in and for Paul.

Those who serve in the public ministry today can also draw on the inexhaustible strength of that Lord whom they serve to give them the ability and the faithfulness they need to carry out their ministry. Let us all pray that the Lord will continue to raise up and call into the public ministry faithful servants who, like Paul, will willingly spend themselves for the Lord and his church. And may we on our part ever appreciate such a ministry as it is carried out among us and support that ministry by hearing the public preaching and teaching of the gospel and honoring those who serve us in the gospel ministry.

Paul's desire to lead believers to full spiritual maturity targeted some very specific areas of concern among the Colossians. The apostle regarded the spiritual challenge those believers were facing as a particularly serious one, and he wanted to help them overcome it. In his ministry he was strenuously exerting himself also for the believers at Laodicea, to whom this letter was also to be read. Paul had never visited Colosse or Laodicea to do mission work. Most of the Christians there were not personally known to him. Nevertheless, Paul wanted them to know about his love for them and his concern for their souls.

His Christian love and his prayers were not reserved only for Christians in congregations he had founded or visited.

They embraced all believers everywhere. The very fact that he wrote this epistle shows his concern for the Christians of the Lycus Valley. Even as he wrote, he was wrestling for their souls in earnest prayers before the Lord. He wanted to encourage them and secure their hearts in Christ by once more holding before them Jesus, the all-sufficient Savior, as the unchanging object of their trust and the source of all the help they would ever need.

By holding Christ before them, Paul wanted first of all to encourage the believers in Colosse and Laodicea in their faith. He wanted them to put aside all doubt and wavering and cling exclusively to Jesus as the Lord of their hearts and of their lives. By encouraging them in their faith the apostle also hoped to unite their hearts more firmly in the love that results from faith. In unity there is strength. Believers united in faith and love and in a firm stand on God's word are more able than isolated believers to detect and combat the errors that threaten their faith.

As they grew in faith and love, Paul promised, the congregations in Colosse and Laodicea would have the riches of complete understanding. Their members would come to an ever deeper knowledge of Jesus as their Savior and Lord. The longer and the more diligently Christians search the Scriptures, the more firmly they will be grounded in the knowledge of God's will and the more they will understand that all the fullness of God's spiritual riches is found in Jesus Christ alone.

The false teachers troubling the Colossians tried to minimize Christ. They boasted of their own wisdom and knowledge and of the powers of the spirits and the angels they worshiped, but neither man nor angel nor any other creature has anything to offer which cannot be found in incomparably superior measure in Christ. In Christ all the treasures of wisdom and knowledge are hidden, not to remain hidden, but to be found in him. Believers who have come to know Christ through the gospel are spiritually rich, and they have true knowledge. All claims of wisdom, knowledge and spiritual treasures apart from Christ are phony and false.

Paul concludes this section, therefore, with a plea to his readers who will always have to contend with false teachers not to be deceived by the fine-sounding arguments of men, but to stand firm on the riches they possess in Christ. Again he reminds his original readers that, though he is physically absent from them and has never met most of them, they are with him always in his thoughts and prayers. And, though he does not minimize the danger that is threatening them, the apostle is also gratified because the gospel is continuing to produce fruit in their congregation.

The false teachers were doing their utmost to destroy the Colossians' faith, but on the whole the believers in Colosse had remained unmoved from their foundation on Christ. No schism, no disorderly behavior had appeared in the congregation. For the most part the Colossians were exhibiting a sterling, steadfast faith. Over this the apostle rejoiced, and he urged them to continue to stand firm in that gospel-based, Christ-centered faith.

May we also heed his encouragement, so that we stand firm against all false teachers and continue to grow in Christ until our hopes are all realized and our knowledge is made perfect in the glory of eternity.

The All-Sufficient Christ
Gives Freedom from Human Regulations

6So then, just as you received Christ Jesus as Lord, continue to live in him, 7rooted and built up in him, strengthened in the faith as you were taught, and overflowing with thankfulness.

8See to it that no one takes you captive through hollow and deceptive philosophy, which depends on human tradition and the basic principles of this world rather than on Christ.

⁹**For in Christ all the fullness of the Deity lives in bodily form,** ¹⁰**and you have been given fullness in Christ, who is the head over every power and authority.** ¹¹**In him you were also circumcised, in the putting off of the sinful nature, not with a circumcision done by the hands of men but with the circumcision done by Christ,** ¹²**having been buried with him in baptism and raised with him through your faith in the power of God, who raised him from the dead.**

¹³**When you were dead in your sins and in the uncircumcision of your sinful nature, God made you alive with Christ. He forgave us all our sins,** ¹⁴**having canceled the written code, with its regulations, that was against us and that stood opposed to us; he took it away, nailing it to the cross.** ¹⁵**And having disarmed the powers and authorities, he made a public spectacle of them, triumphing over them by the cross.**

Paul has eloquently spoken of the greatness of the Lord Jesus and of the immensity and completeness of the spiritual blessings that believers have in him. He has reminded the Colossians that the great purpose of his ministry was to preach that all-sufficient Christ. Paul closed the previous section by complimenting the Colossians on their firm stand in Christ. Now, in what is really the main message of the epistle, he urges them to continue in that firm stand. This encouragement comes in both positive and negative forms in verses 6-8, then moves on to another inspiring description of our all-sufficient Savior in verses 9-15.

The apostle was pleased by the reports Epaphras had brought him about the Colossians' firm stand in Christ, but the false teachers were challenging that stand every day. Paul was concerned about the Colossians' spiritual depth, so he encouraged them, "Just as you received Christ Jesus as Lord, continue to live in him." The Colossians had heard the gospel from Epaphras and believed it, embracing Jesus with a Spirit-given faith.

When they came to faith, Jesus came to live in their hearts. They lived in intimate fellowship with him, and they needed to continue to live in Jesus. They needed to live in conscious awareness of his presence in their hearts and lives. They needed to go forward in connection with Christ, trusting his word, cherishing his forgiveness, obeying his commandments and guarding against everything that might disrupt their blessed relationship with him.

With four brief phrases the apostle expands on what he means by "continue to live in him" As he does, he suggests to us the key qualities of a life in Christ. When the Spirit first led them to faith in Jesus, the Colossians were *rooted* in Christ. They were implanted in Jesus as their all-sufficient Savior. Now they needed to continue to draw strength and nourishment from him, sending their roots of faith down ever deeper into Jesus and his word, as a tree sends its roots deeper into the soil to draw nourishment from the earth. The more Christians use God's word and the sacraments, the deeper they sink their roots of faith into Christ. The more firmly they are rooted in Christ, the less likely they are to be blown over by the storms of false teaching and the fierce winds of the troubles and sorrows of life.

When he brought them to faith in Jesus, the Holy Spirit established the Colossians on Jesus. Jesus is the firm foundation on which the constantly growing structure of believers' faith and life rests. On that foundation the Colossians are to be *built up*. They are to grow in their faith and progress in their Christian living, like a building rising higher and higher as it progresses to its completion.

Sending their roots of faith down into Christ and being built upward on Christ will result in their being *strengthened* in the faith. Their spiritual knowledge and their hold on Christ, in whom all the treasures of wisdom and knowledge are hidden, will be strengthened. Their faith will be constantly confirmed. They will become ever more firmly convinced that no new doctrines or directions for their spiritual lives are necessary, because they have all that they need in Christ.

For all the blessings which result in the spiritual conditions here described, Paul urges the Colossians to *overflow with thankfulness*. As believers view their spiritual blessings from the perspective of a living, growing faith, their thanksgiving will overflow and rush forth in mighty streams into every area of their lives. Christians who are rooted and built up in Christ and daily strengthened in faith in him cannot help but be thankful, and they will cheerfully and lovingly make that thankfulness evident in their words and actions every day.

Positively, continuing in Christ means for believers all that the apostle has held before us in verse 7. Negatively, it means not letting oneself be carried away by human teachings that do not honor Christ or recognize the all-sufficiency of what he has done for man's salvation. Such errors were being promoted by false teachers in Colosse. Paul did not want the believers there to be misled by their clever arguments.

The apostle never dignifies the "Colossian heresy" by describing all its features, but from what he says here in verses 8 and 9 and also in verses 16, 18 and 20 of this same chapter we conclude that this false doctrine was a rather clever and devious mixture of Jewish ideas and pagan philosophy. Those who promoted this false teaching claimed that it was a "more complete" form of Christianity.

For all its wisdom and supposed sophistication, the "Colossian heresy" failed to acknowledge the all-sufficiency of Christ. At the very moment Paul penned these words he knew that those false teachers with their Christ-denying errors were trying to make the Colossian believers their prey and lead them away as captives. Paul's advice to the besieged Colossians is simple: Don't let the false teachers succeed. You belong to Christ. Don't let anyone else kidnap you by false teaching and make you his spiritual slaves.

The enemies of the gospel were trying to take the Colossians' souls captive by a religious system based, not on divine revelation, but on human reasoning. This system claimed to offer explanations of divine things according to ideas generally acceptable to men. It was no doubt cleverly presented by its proponents. Perhaps they were even sincere about it. It seemed both logical and learned, as do many systems of religious thoughts and morals invented and proposed by human beings.

Nevertheless this religious system and all others like it are not only hollow and empty; they are dangerous and deceptive. They are invented by men and used by men for their own purposes. Those who propose such teachings and systems and traditions are like traders in fake stock. They try to persuade people to surrender valuable stock in exchange for something worthless.

The phrase, "the basic principles of the world," is probably best understood to mean the elementary religious ideas of sinful human beings by which both Jews and Gentiles vainly tried to earn God's favor. Such false ideas have lurked within the sin-blinded hearts of human beings since the fall. They enslave people to earthly laws, customs and traditions. To these basic principles of this world they or their teachers attach the idea of merit. Thus they attempt to pay for sin and to set things right between themselves and God by their own efforts. The Colossian false teachers were presenting notions about things like circumcision, festivals, food and drink and the worship of angels as ways of achieving salvation, or at least a "more complete" Christianity. The false teachers represented their ideas as a more sophisticated form of Christianity. They looked down with haughty disdain on those who held to the "simple" gospel of salvation by grace through faith in Jesus.

It's that way today, too. Many modern teachers of religion present what seem to be sophisticated and clever systems of belief, complete with impressive-sounding terminology and logical explanations. They, too, look down on those who hold to the simple gospel and put their trust in a verbally inspired Bible. They regard them as intellectually deprived and spiritually naive, but here Paul dismisses all human religious speculation as hollow and deceptive philosophy. He makes it clear that those who propose clever human religious systems are captives to the elementary religious ideas of the unconverted world.

In marked contrast to such hollow and deceptive philosophy the apostle sets forth the all-sufficient Lord Jesus Christ. He reminds his readers that in Christ alone all fullness dwells, and in Christ alone believers themselves are made full. The statement in verse 9, "In Christ all the fullness of the Deity lives in bodily form," is another key doctrinal statement in the New Testament dealing with the person of Christ. Very simply, yet very powerfully, it tells us that Jesus is both God and man in one person. It tells us that all the characteristics that belong to God dwell in Christ, not only as the Son of God, but also as the Son of man. When Jesus took on a human nature, the fullness of the Godhead was actually contained within his person and within his body.

Human reason rebels at the idea that within the human Christ that men could see, was contained, and still is contained, all the fullness of the majesty of God. That is something like saying that all the water in the ocean is contained in a pitcher held in one's hand. Nevertheless, that is exactly what the Bible says when it tells us that all the fullness of the Deity dwells in Christ.

It is evident from Scripture that Jesus was a man. He was like every other man in stature, appearance, habits and needs. It is also evident from Scripture that God is extraordinary. He is eternal and present everywhere. He is all-knowing, all-powerful, all-wise. He is all goodness and love. Yet in the human nature of Christ are contained all the extraordinary characteristics, yes, the very substance and being of God. When Jesus was conceived in the womb of Mary, God himself took on human nature and became man. When Jesus died on the cross, God died. The body and blood that bought our redemption did so because all the divine fullness dwelt in the human nature of Christ.

This truth is a divine mystery. It is something that we cannot even begin to comprehend with our sin-limited human reason. But it is something we know and believe, because God clearly reveals it to us in passages of his word like this one. Such inspired words of Scripture assure us beyond all doubt that Jesus Christ, the God-man, is our all-sufficient Savior and Lord. Since all the fullness of the Deity dwells in Christ, he is the all-sufficient Savior, and we can find all that we need for our spiritual fullness and complete salvation in him.

When we by faith are connected with a Savior in whom all fullness dwells, we, too, are filled to the limit. We have all that we need for time and eternity, the fullness of every spiritual blessing. We have no need for human philosophies or schemes that are developed in accord with the elements of this world. None of these traditions, philosophies or schemes could ever add a single thing to that which Jesus has already made complete. In things divine, addition is always subtraction. When human beings try to add to the completeness found in Christ, they lose. Only to those who abide in the all-sufficient Christ and in him alone will the blessings of his fullness flow.

Christ's fullness and sufficiency also include his absolute rule over every power and authority in the spirit world. As part of their complicated religious system, the errorists in

Colosse seem to have taught that spiritual beings (powers and authorities) could somehow affect believers' lives apart from Christ. We know they advocated the worship of angels (see 2:18). Paul counters this false speculation by reminding his readers of the truth he has already set before them in chapter 1:15, the truth that Christ is the supreme Lord over all created beings, including those that inhabit the spirit world.

Apart from Christ good angels cannot help believers, and with Christ they will not be harmed by evil angels. So why should Christians look for something more or try to add to what the Savior offers, when in him they already have everything they need? The false teachers said, "You need Jesus — plus." Paul says, "You need Jesus — period." In Jesus believers have complete fullness and need fear no power in heaven or on earth or under the earth.

Some of the ideas being promoted by the false teachers in Colosse were obviously Judaistic in character. We met the Judaizers in this volume once before, in connection with our study of Philippians 3, especially verses 1-6. These were Pharisees with a Christian label. They insisted that believing in Jesus was not enough for salvation. Christians also had to observe certain of the outward laws and ceremonies that Moses gave to the Old Testament Israelites. Like the Judaizers in Philippi, the false teachers in Colosse put a great deal of emphasis on the ceremony of circumcision. Paul's remarks in verses 16 and 17 of this chapter indicate that they also called for adherence to Old Testament dietary restrictions and strict observance of Old Testament festivals and Sabbath laws.

By insisting on these things, these teachers claimed that they were supplementing Christ's work and thus making themselves better, more complete Christians, but in reality they were trying to establish and fill a need where there was none. They were like beggars, who claimed that they had a good business opportunity for people who were already wealthier than they were.

Paul refutes those who insist on circumcision as a condition for salvation by reminding the Colossians, as he reminded the Philippians, that believers in Jesus possess a vastly superior circumcision not done with hands. By insisting on physical circumcision as an outward ritual which should supplement Christ's work, the Colossian errorists had reduced circumcision to what Paul calls in Philippians a "mutilation," a mere physical operation. There was absolutely no promise of God connected with it.

The circumcision that believers receive is a spiritual thing. It is a truly beneficial and blessed putting off of their old, sinful nature through the work of the Holy Spirit in their hearts. When the Spirit brings believers to faith in Jesus, their old, sinful nature, like a filthy garment, is cut off and thrown away. Then the dominant force in believers' lives is the new nature created by the Spirit, a nature which loves God and seeks to serve him. Because they have this new nature, believers' physical members are no longer instruments of sin, but instruments of righteousness for God.

As long as believers live on earth, the old nature will continue to lurk within them and try to regain its mastery over their lives. But the Holy Spirit, who gave believers their new nature, daily renews and strengthens that nature through the power of the gospel. Thus he enables believers to defeat the sinful nature with its lusts and desires. What was a mere physical operation like circumcision by comparison with the spiritual operation which the Holy Spirit had already performed within the hearts of the Colossians?

The Colossians had received this spiritual circumcision, Paul says, in baptism. Incidentally, by making the connection between Old Testament circumcision and New Testament baptism here, Paul indicates that in the New Testament baptism has taken the place of circumcision. The Old Testament circumcision, as God gave it to Abraham, was a sacrament, a means of grace by which God made the male children members of the covenant line and sharers in the covenant promises God made to Abraham. Those covenant promises centered in the Savior from sin that God promised to send from Abraham's descendants.

When Christ came, he fulfilled all those covenant promises. Before he ascended into heaven, he gave baptism to his New Testament Church. When they were baptized, Paul assures his readers, they were buried and raised with Christ through faith. Jesus died and was buried as the substitute for all mankind. The sins of the whole human race were nailed with him to his cross and buried with him in his tomb. He bore the punishment that satisfied the Father's divine justice, and on Easter morning God raised him up in that great declaration that his atonement had been accepted and the world was saved.

In baptism, Paul says, the Colossians had been made personal sharers in all of that. Through baptism they had been brought to faith or strengthened in the faith that personally joined each of them to Christ. Through baptism each one had personally received the blessings Christ had won for them. By virtue of their union with Christ in baptism God regarded Christ's death and burial and resurrection as if they were each individual believer's own death and burial and resurrection. Through baptism the Colossian believers' sin-laden natures had been crucified and buried with Christ, and a new nature created by the Holy Spirit in God's image had arisen in their hearts. Their status had been changed from objects of God's wrath to members of his spiritual household. All these blessings and more were spiritual blessings bestowed by Christ, transmitted to individual believers through baptism and received by faith.

Again, what a contrast there was between this blessed spiritual circumcision connected with the promises of God and the outward, mechanical circumcision advocated by the false teachers. That circumcision was performed on the body, and its supposed merits were connected with no divine promise but only with the deceptive religious theories of men. New Testament believers have no need for circumcision as a religious rite or a meritorious act, and they should not be intimidated by those who claim they do. New Testament believers, by virtue of their being baptized into Christ, have received a far better circumcision, the spiritual circumcision of heart and life.

In a genuine spirit of Christian jubilation Paul expands on that same thought in verse 13. In their natural spiritual state the Colossians, together with all human beings since the fall, were morally and spiritually dead. Their thoughts and desires, as well as their words and actions, were completely opposed to God and his word and will. In this condition they were spiritually impotent and totally unable to help themselves. They deserved only God's wrath and condemnation.

But God's amazing grace did not leave the Colossians in their lost and helpless state. Ponder this, Paul encourages them. Continue to reflect on it. Upon you, deeply fallen and utterly, hopelessly lost; upon you Gentiles, no less than on the Jews, his chosen people of Old Testament times, God's grace has been bestowed. God, who raised Christ from the dead, has raised you from the death of spiritual ignorance and unbelief and made you spiritually alive with Christ.

If sinners are to be made spiritually alive, their sin and guilt must be removed in God's sight. To do this, Paul says, "He forgave all our sins." Forgiveness is God's bountiful, unmerited gift. Paul's subtle change from the pronoun "you" in the first part of verse 13 to "us" in the last part of that same verse is worth noting. In Christ

God has forgiven the whole world of sinners, and Paul cannot talk about so great a subject without including himself. He, too, had experienced God's forgiveness. He, too, had been made alive in Christ and rescued from eternal damnation. God's forgiveness stood at the very center of his life. It stands at the center of every believer's life. Every believer is included in the "we" of this sentence.

In forgiving sinners and making them alive God canceled the written code with its regulations that stood against us. The written code is the written law of God, the divine decrees with their uncompromising "Thou shalt" and "Thou shalt not." No doubt Paul is here thinking both of the moral law, the unchangeable will of God for human behavior that applies to people of all times, as well as the Mosaic Ceremonial laws, which included the laws God gave to the Old Testament Israelites concerning foods, festivals and circumcision.

That written code, Paul says, was against us. In both its moral and ceremonial character the law demanded a perfection no human being could achieve. It set forth a way of salvation impossible for human beings to attain. So it stood as man's accuser. But in Christ God canceled that written code. He took away its demanding, curse-pronouncing character. He took it and nailed it with Christ to the cross.

When Christ died, the law as man's accuser also died. The historical purpose of the Mosaic laws was fulfilled. Their very necessity was brought to an end. On the cross Christ paid the punishment that a world of sinners deserved because of their transgressions of God's moral law, the curse of eternal death.

If the law had not died in the blood of his cross, Christ could not have risen. But he did rise, thereby guaranteeing forever that the law as our accuser is dead and gone and spiritual quickening and resurrection are ours. Our debt of sin and guilt has been canceled. At the foot of the cross we find deliverance and life. This does not mean, of course, that God's unchangeable moral law has lost all significance for believers or that believers can now forget about loving God and their neighbor. No, the moral law still serves as a perfect mirror, daily showing also Christians their sins and their need for the Savior's forgiveness.

In their Christian lives of service to their Savior believers use the moral law as the perfect standard and guide, but the law as a code of rules and regulations that demands perfection and pronounces curses on imperfect sinners has been wiped out and removed by the power of Christ's cross. All who are joined to Christ by faith need no longer fear the law's threats and curses. Nor can they be bullied by those who try to make the law their accuser again by making the keeping of a written code a condition for salvation.

When Christ, by his successful atoning work, brought about the death of the law as man's accuser, he also disarmed the powers and authorities, the wicked spirits about whom the false teachers were so concerned. These evil hordes, led by Satan, brought sin into God's perfect world. They plunged humanity into sin at the fall.

They still tempt man to sin, and then, when sinners have fallen, these evil spirits turn around and accuse them before God. They are at war with God and believers and arrogantly try to usurp the powers that belong to God. These evil spirits are powerful and devious. The Colossians, who were being troubled by all sorts of strange and frightful teachings concerning the spirit world, needed to know that Jesus had disarmed all those evil powers and authorities.

As man's substitute he overcame the devil's temptations in the desert. He won victory upon victory over the hosts of demons throughout his ministry, and on Calvary, when the evil powers had their dark hour and did their worst, Christ administered the final blow, stripping the devil and his hosts forever of the power to accuse sinners before God.

Then "he made a public spectacle of them, triumphing over them by the cross." In the days of the apostles the Roman emperors or senate often granted a victorious general a grand triumph upon his return to Rome. There would be a procession through the streets of the city. The general, together with his legions, marched proudly, and the captives and spoils they had taken were displayed. In the triumph of which the apostle speaks here, the defeated powers of hell are made to march as chained captives, as a result of Christ's victory on the cross.

We take this statement of the apostle to refer to Christ's descent into hell. Here and in 1 Peter 3:18,19 Scripture indicates that, after Christ was made alive, he descended into hell and publicly proclaimed his absolute, complete and final victory over the devil and his hellish hosts. He publicly put them to shame.

This, in turn, assures us believers that the devils and evil spirits have no real power over us. Yes, they are still our enemies. They are still powerful and dangerous, and we must daily beware of them and struggle against them. But Christ, our all-sufficient Savior, has defeated Satan and all his forces. Because we share in his victory by faith, we have in him the power to defeat the devil's hosts, too.

16Therefore do not let anyone judge you by what you eat or drink, or with regard to a religious festival, a New Moon celebration or a Sabbath day. 17These are a shadow of the things that were to come; the reality, however, is found in Christ. 18Do not let anyone who delights in false humility and the worship of angels disqualify you for the prize. Such a person goes into great detail about what he has seen, and his unspiritual mind puffs him up with idle notions. 19He has lost connection with the Head, from whom the whole body, supported and held together by its ligaments and sinews, grows as God causes it to grow.

20Since you died with Christ to the basic principles of this world, why, as though you still belonged to it, do you submit to its rules: 21"Do not handle! Do not taste! Do not touch!"? 22These are all destined to perish with use, because they are based on human commands and teachings. 23Such regulations indeed have an appearance of wisdom, with their self-imposed worship, their false humility and their harsh treatment of the body, but they lack any value in restraining sensual indulgence.

The apostle continues his forceful attack on the various features of the deceptive philosophy with which the false teachers are trying to carry the Colossian believers away as captives. Paul moves easily back and forth among the Jewish and pagan features of this false teaching, indicating that those ideas have been cleverly woven together by those who are promoting them. But one by one Paul blows away each feature of the false teaching by confronting it with the sufficiency of Christ.

Earlier in this chapter Paul referred to Judaistic features of the Colossian false teaching by mentioning the false teachers' insistence on the outward act of circumcision. The Judaizers, of whom we spoke in that verse, also placed great emphasis on the keeping of written rules and law codes. Now in verses 16 and 17 the apostle condemns another obviously Judaistic feature of the Colossian error, the insistence that the keeping of certain Old Testament laws and ceremonies, particularly laws concerning foods and festivals, had to be added to faith in Christ if believers were to have complete salvation.

Within the sinful heart of every human being there lurks a spiritual pride that refuses to admit that he is totally helpless spiritually and totally incapable of contributing anything to his own salvation. Human pride stubbornly insists on believing that sinners can do something, however small and insignificant it may be, to earn favor with God and to help save themselves.

This pride leads sinners to disregard the real purpose of God's law and to regard an outward keeping of the law as a means for salvation. It also leads human beings, in their perverse and sinful way of thinking, to set up their own laws and rules and schemes and to imagine that the keeping of these human laws and rules makes them better people and somehow merits them favor with God. This type of thinking can be found at the heart of every non-Christian religion that has ever appeared on earth. All too often, it can be found perverting the thinking also of those who claim to believe in Jesus, honor the true God and respect his word.

In Old Testament times the Lord lamented through Isaiah, "Their worship of me is made up only of rules taught by men." The Pharisees of Jesus' day claimed to be the guardians of the Scriptures, but in reality they placed their own laws and traditions above the Scriptures and taught that by keeping their laws people could achieve holiness before God.

The early Christian church had the Judaizers. In the Middle Ages the gospel of God's free grace was obscured by the laws and traditions, canons and decrees of the church of Rome. Today we have the cults who claim that certain outward observances and laws have to be added to faith in Christ if a person is to be saved. We have the "two-tiered" Christianity which separates Christians who have had the "conversion experience" from those who have not. False teachings spawned by man's sinful pride are in evidence all around us.

Sometimes we are inclined to raise our cherished Christian customs and traditions to the level of laws. We may try to impose them on others or try to make each other "better" Christians by proposing as a guide for our lives laws that go beyond what God gives us in his moral law. The problem

Paul addresses here, therefore, is a practical one also for the Christian church of the twentieth century. It is one thing to claim to believe in Jesus as the Savior. It is quite another to truly honor him by acknowledging his fullness, his total completeness and all-sufficiency as our Savior and the Savior of all the world.

With regard to the false teachers' claim that the keeping of Old Testament laws and ceremonies needed to be added to faith, Paul tells the Colossian Christians not to let anyone judge their Christianity on the basis of these things. Those who taught that the New Testament Christians had to keep certain Mosaic laws and ceremonies did not understand the real reason God gave those laws. God never intended the laws concerning diets, festivals, ceremonies and sabbaths to be ways to salvation. No sinner can save himself by keeping any law, because no sinner can keep any law perfectly. When sinners realize this they will despair of God's laws as the way of salvation. They will see them instead as a perfect mirror, which shows their sinfulness.

The civil and ceremonial laws that God gave through Moses also had a historical purpose, namely, to keep his chosen Old Testament people, the Israelites, separate and distinct from the unbelieving nations around them, until God's promises were fulfilled and Christ arrived.

They were to serve as shadows, pictures of the coming Savior. If the sun is behind a person that person's shadow will arrive at the destination before he does, and it will prove that the person casting the shadow is coming. All the elaborate features of the Old Testament laws of Moses were intended to remind the Israelites of God's great promise to send a Savior and to make them all the more eager for the Savior's coming.

When Paul wrote this epistle, Jesus had come. The temporary shadows had served their purpose. The reality had arrived. Jesus is the real bread of life, the perfect passover lamb, the perfect sacrifice that really atoned for sin, the bringer of the true sabbath rest for the souls of men. Every Old Testament law, ceremony and shadow had been fulfilled in him. What further purpose could those shadows serve? How foolish it was, therefore, for the false teachers to insist on embracing those shadows while they were ignoring Jesus, the body who cast the shadow.

It was not wrong, of course, for Jewish believers to continue to observe some of their Old Testament ceremonial laws simply as customs, but it was wrong to insist on those customs and to make them laws for New Testament believers. It was wrong to ascribe to them a value they did not have and to impose them on New Testament Christians as conditions for being saved. Such teaching denied the all-sufficiency of Jesus and his redemptive work. It placed an unbearable burden on believers. And it endangered their very salvation by promoting a religion, not of grace and faith and Christ, but of human laws and rules.

Christians today, too, must beware of any attempts to bind consciences with human laws, customs and rules. Any teaching that seeks to supplement what Christ has done with what man can do is dangerous and soul-destroying folly. We must reject such teachings, because they fail to give all glory to Christ.

"False humility and the worship of angels" was another element in the teaching that Paul condemns. Again, we wish we had more information about the exact nature of the teaching. No doubt the Colossian believers understood exactly what Paul was talking about. All we know for certain is that this aspect of the false teaching, too, was a human opinion that denied the sufficiency of Christ.

The worship of angels probably resulted from a mixture of Jewish and heathen religious ideas, curiosity and superstition. The Greek world was fascinated by the unknown, and all human beings are naturally superstitious. Elaborate theories about the unknown spirit world could easily have caught the fancy of both Jews and Greeks whose intellectual pride regarded the gospel as too simple. The records of the early church in the general area of Colosse and Laodicea indicate that false teachings about worshiping angels and spirits posed a real problem for the church.

But what about the false humility the apostle mentions here? Again, we can only speculate. It seems reasonable to assume that the false teachers justified their worship of angels by claiming in "false humility" that, since they were unworthy of going to God directly, they could perhaps go to him through angels instead. This reasonable sounding idea of going to God through created beings, including believers who have already entered heaven, is still spooking around in certain Christian churches. But no matter how reasonable this teaching sounds, it is a human idea only, and it is false, because it denies the sufficiency of Christ as the only mediator between God and man. Don't let those who propose such theories disqualify you for the prize, Paul tells the Colossians. Don't let them make you feel unfit or unworthy or inferior because you believe the "simple" gospel. For it is in the simple gospel alone, and not in clever, human speculation, that Jesus, the all-sufficient Savior, can be found.

The false teachers in Colosse based their theories about false humility and the worship of angels on special revelations they claimed to have received and a superior knowledge of the spirit world they claimed to have. In connection with those boastful claims they sought to impose still more laws, restrictions and rules on those who followed them. With lofty scorn these teachers looked down on those who held to the simple gospel. They thrust themselves forward as wiser, more sophisticated Christians. They boasted about their humility (how ironic that was!), and they suffered from an inflated sense of their own importance.

Paul was not impressed by the claims of the false teachers. Nor was he impressed with their "sophisticated" Christianity. Their elaborate teachings were nothing but the products of unspiritual minds which had lost connection with Christ. Those false teachers failed to see that real spiritual wisdom and life and all true spiritual treasures can be found in Christ alone, not in the worship of angels or speculation about the spirit world or sophisticated religious systems with elaborate rules.

Christ is the Head of the church. Believers are his body. The growth and the functions of a body are normally dictated by the head. Just as a human body, when it is properly supported and held together by its joints and ligaments, experiences normal growth, so the church, blessed by God, will grow in grace and knowledge and Christian living through Christ, its Head. The church owes its salvation, its very existence to Christ. All its growth must come from Christ. It need not and must not seek any other source of salvation or any other source of strength to overcome sin or to increase in knowledge, virtue and joy. Believers have all that they need and all that they want in Jesus alone. Every teaching that denies this or fails to find its sufficiency in Christ is valueless and deceitful and severs people's connection with Christ, the Head, whether they still claim to believe in him or not.

In baptism believers have been buried with Christ. They have been joined to Christ and made personal sharers in his death and resurrection. By virtue of this union with Christ they receive new spiritual life in which they are set free from the crude religious beliefs devised by fallen human beings and the false hopes for salvation based on human merit and earthly law codes.

In Christ, New Testament believers have also been set free from the heavy yoke of the Old Testament laws of Moses. But if, after receiving this new life of freedom and the fullness of salvation in Christ, the Colossian believers began to listen to the false teachers; if they began to follow their rules and to believe that by keeping those rules they were earning or supplementing their salvation, they would be returning again to the very condition from which they had been delivered by Christ. That would be the worst of all spiritual fates.

With stinging ridicule Paul sums up those regulations to which the false teachers were trying to enslave them: "Do not handle! Do not taste! Do not touch!" Why submit to all those regulations, he asks, as if by enough "don'ts" you could obtain the victory over sin? Food, drink and all the other things in the world are given to Christians to use in the world, and they perish with that use. Is it not foolish to base the hope for victory over sin, or even for salvation itself, on man-made ordinances based on the use or non-use of perishable things? How can Christians, who have come to know Jesus and his all-sufficient salvation, let themselves be deceived into substituting those wretched and spiritually destructive human teachings for the teachings of Christ?

Yes, the self-imposed rituals, the worship of angels, the false humility and self-denial practiced by the false teachers made a great impression on some people. How serious and godly those who practiced these things appeared. The very nature and urgency of the apostle's concern here shows that at least some of the Colossian believers must have wondered whether those teachers did, after all, have something to offer. So Paul concludes this section by setting everything once more in its proper perspective.

Such regulations, he says, have the appearance of wisdom. But that is all they have. They lead, not toward Christ and salvation, but away from him and to destruction. Such human teachings have no value in overcoming sin. Those who follow them do nothing but indulge their own pride. True Christianity is not something that can be reduced to a set of rules, nor does it indulge sinful human beings or flatter their pride. True Christianity is being in Christ, rooted and built up in him, buried, made alive and raised with him, walking with him and living with him.

Yes, we Christians will use God's moral law as a guide for our lives. Its perfection is the goal for which we constantly strive, but our striving to keep the law has absolutely nothing to do with gaining our salvation. Rather, it is the result of our being saved, the thankful expression of a faith that has found all its sufficiency in Christ. "The life I live in the body," Paul tells the Galatians (2:20), "I live by faith in the Son of God, who loved me and gave himself for me."

JESUS IS SUFFICIENT
FOR OUR CHRISTIAN LIVES
COLOSSIANS 3:1 — 4:18

The All-Sufficient Christ Gives Power for Holy Living

3 Since, then, you have been raised with Christ, set your hearts on things above, where Christ is seated at the right hand of God. ²Set your minds on things above, not on earthly things. ³For you died, and your life is now hidden with Christ in God. ⁴When Christ, who is your life, appears, then you also will appear with him in glory.

⁵Put to death, therefore, whatever belongs to your earthly nature: sexual immorality, impurity, lust, evil desire and greed, which is idolatry. ⁶Because of these, the wrath of God is coming. ⁷ You used to walk in these ways, in the life you once lived. ⁸But now you must rid yourselves of all such things as these: anger, rage, malice, slander, and filthy language from your lips. ⁹Do not lie to each other, since you have taken off your old self with its practices ¹⁰and have put on the new self, which is being renewed in knowledge in the image of its Creator. ¹¹Here there is no Greek or Jew, circumcised or uncircumcised, barbarian, Scythian, slave or free, but Christ is all, and is in all.

The apostle has concluded the doctrinal portion of his epistle. He has dealt quite directly and thoroughly with the false teachings that were threatening the Colossians, confronting the various elements of that false teaching with the all-sufficiency of Christ. Now, as he does also in many of his other epistles, Paul follows the doctrinal portion with a practical section, giving the Colossians encouragement and advice for their day-to-day Christian living. As he does, he shows all Christians the vital importance of the connection between what Christians believe and how they live. He shows that, just as Christ is all-sufficient for believers' faith, he is also all-sufficient for their Christian lives.

In chapter 2:12, Paul introduced the thought that in baptism Christians are buried and raised with Christ. He repeats that thought here and uses it as the basic, motivating truth for all the following encouragements to Christian living. Believers have been raised with Christ. Their faith rests, not on a dead and lifeless Savior, but on a living Lord, who rose from the dead and ascended into heaven. He now sits at God's right hand and rules as the exalted God-man over the universe, filling all things with his power.

Christ's resurrection and exaltation are the guarantee of his lordship and of believers' forgiveness. But even more, it is something which brings about a spiritual resurrection in believers' hearts. When the Holy Spirit brings people to faith, he joins them to Christ and makes them personal sharers in Christ's death and resurrection. God regards Christ's death as if it were the individual believer's death and credits it to each one. He raises each one from spiritual death to spiritual life, setting him free from the power of sin and bestowing peace, joy and forgiveness on him in Christ.

Believers have been made personal sharers in the blessings earned by Christ, and now they are spiritually alive and joined to Christ. This ought to motivate them to live a special kind of life, a life lived in and for Christ. Those who are risen with Christ should be so transformed and changed inwardly that they will set their hearts on things above. Things above are heavenly things, spiritual treasures, the blessings that the risen and ascended Christ won for sinners and which he graciously bestows on those who come to him. Those treasures include forgiveness, spiritual knowledge, faith, and all the fruits that faith produces in a Christian's

life, beginning with love. Such treasures, and not the changeable treasures of the world, are now to be the real concerns
of believers raised with Christ. Christians' goals, values and
decisions ought to reflect a conscious heavenly-mindedness.

That does not mean that Christians will forget about their
duties in this life or fail to fulfill the earthly tasks the Lord
has assigned to them. Nor does it mean that they will with-
draw from the earthly society in which the Lord has placed
them. It does mean that, as they live their day-to-day lives in
the world, they will always take into account that their real
citizenship is in heaven. They will never lose sight of the
truth that nothing on earth is a lasting treasure, but that
lasting values can be found only in Christ.

Many of the Christians to whom Paul originally wrote
this letter had been won for Christianity from the heathen
world. There were temptations all around them to turn their
backs on their Christian values and their Christian way of
life and return to the kind of living that satisfied their sinful
desires. But Paul reminds us that all who truly understand
what Christ has done for them and know the meaning of his
life and death, resurrection and ascension, will not be able to
center their lives again on the useless, changeable, material
things and the sinful way of living about which others are so
concerned. Believers will center their lives on their risen and
ascended Lord. Since Christ has ascended and sits at God's
right hand as the ruler of the universe, believers can set their
hearts on heavenly treasures. They can have the absolute
confidence that their exalted Savior will pour down on them
the gifts and blessings they need to build their lives on him.

When the Holy Spirit brings people to faith in Christ, they
die to their sinful selves and their old, earthly way of living.
Their guilt-laden natures are buried with Christ. Their status is changed from objects of condemnation to members of

167

God's family of believers, and they enter upon a whole new way of life in Christ. During this present life that new life is hidden with Christ in God. The inner nature of that life is not something that can be seen. It is a spiritual thing. Already in this life believers experience the benefits of peace with God and the blessings of his forgiveness in their hearts, and their new lives in Christ are reflected in their outward actions.

To the world that does not seem like much. Unbelievers may laugh and call believers foolish for adopting a life-style that rejects the world's standards and values and claims an invisible connection with a divine Lord. Believers experience many of the same physical troubles that unbelievers experience in the world. But when the ascended Lord returns again as Judge of all the world, what is now hidden from the world will be made gloriously visible. The glory of the inner relationship believers enjoy with the Savior will be revealed, and they will be displayed in glory with him, a glory they will enjoy perfectly and without interruption for all eternity.

Expanding on the idea of dying to their old way of life, Paul urges believers to give practical evidence of their heavenly-mindedness by putting to death whatever belongs to their earthly nature. In their natural spiritual state, apart from Christ, all human beings since Adam are sinful and the servants of sin. In that condition they devote themselves to the service of sin. When people come to faith, however, they die to that old sinful, earthly way of life and enter a new way of living in Christ. They become heavenly-minded.

Believers still have that old, sinful nature lurking within them, trying to defeat the new, heavenly-minded nature they have from the Holy Spirit. Day after day that old nature tries to regain supremacy in their lives. Believers' lives are a constant struggle between the two natures at war within them, and all too often the old nature succeeds in scoring victories, as Paul so vividly describes it in Romans 7.

That is why, even though they died to sin when they were first brought to faith, it is still necessary for Christians daily to put to death the things that belong to their earthly natures. By virtue of their new lives with Christ believers have the power to put sin to death in their lives. Paul's encouragement here is that Christians daily and consciously strive to use the spiritual power they have in Christ to refuse to devote their bodies and minds to the service of sin.

As part of his encouragement to put sin to death in their lives, Paul provides, by way of example, a list of sins that spring from the sinful nature. He does not spend a great deal of time in sordid descriptions of these sins. He simply cites them as examples of the vices in which the sinful nature is inclined to live, and he urges believers to strive to get rid of them. Included in the apostle's catalog of sins to be put to death daily are sexual immorality, all the sinful actions that transgress the Sixth Commandment; impurity, the addiction to impure things in both the body and the mind; lust, the evil cravings out of which all other sins proceed; evil desires; and greed, the passion for getting things to satisfy our own desires, even if those things have to be gotten in an evil way. Covetousness, Paul reminds us, is really idolatry, because it gives that which is coveted first place in one's life, and faith cannot live in a heart devoted to the love of earthly things.

No doubt Paul selected these particular examples because they were sins especially prevalent in the society in which the Colossians lived. These were sins with which the devil was constantly tempting those who were striving to live for Christ. Such sins are still prominent in our society, because man's sinful nature does not change. So our spiritual lives are under constant attack. We are tempted daily and with the Spirit's help we must strive to put these sins to death in our lives each day.

Human beings often revel in sins such as Paul lists here. In his day sexual sins were encouraged and practiced in connection with the worship of certain heathen gods and goddesses. Today the arousal of evil lust and the participation in sexual sins of every kind is often held up as the ideal. Sexual sins are justified in the name of freedom and self-expression, and greed is simply taken for granted as a way of life. But in verse 6 Paul puts everything in perspective when he says, "Because of these, the wrath of God is coming." Human beings may make gods of sins and glorify them. Society may try to expunge the word "sin" from its vocabulary, but God still sees sin for what it really is, a violation of holiness.

God does not take sin lightly. In his holiness and perfect justice he demands that sin be punished. All who continue in sin and refuse to seek God's forgiveness in Christ Jesus will one day feel the awful wrath of God because of those sins, if not here in time, then surely hereafter in eternity.

Before they were won for Christ, the Colossians lived in the sinful, earthly vices the apostle has just condemned. In that state they had been subject to the wrath of God, but now in Christ they had been set free from that wretched state. Their lives as heathen were behind them, and in their new lives they could put to death the sins and vices that had characterized them before. Once again, therefore, Paul urges them to strive to defeat sin in their lives.

He urges them to rid their lives, not only of the sins that directly disrupt their relationship to God, such as have been mentioned in verse 5, but also of all the acts of lovelessness that disrupt their relationship with their fellow men. Many of these sins are not even regarded as vices by human society, but Christians are to strive to put completely out of their lives things like anger, rage, malice and smoldering resentment against the neighbor, slander, and filthy language of every kind. Special mention is also made of lying, perhaps because it is so common to the sinful nature of mankind and the society in which Christians live, but at the same time completely contrary to everything a Christian ought to stand for and ought to be.

The Colossians ought to put off all the sins he has mentioned, as well as all the other sins that characterize the sinful nature, because that old nature itself has been put off. When Christians are brought to faith, they put off their old nature like an old filthy garment, and they put on the new man, a new nature renewed by the Holy Spirit in the image and knowledge of God. When Adam was created, he possessed the image of God. His soul was holy and sinless. He knew God perfectly and rejoiced to do God's will. When Adam fell into sin, however, he lost the image of God, for both himself and his descendants. Now all human beings are born into the world, not in God's holy image, but in Adam's sinful image.

When the Holy Spirit brings sinners to faith in Jesus through the gospel he recreates that lost image of God in their hearts. As long as believers live here on earth, however, their sinful nature clings to them, constantly opposing and battling against the new nature, constantly seeking to reassert its authority in believers' lives — and often succeeding. Daily, therefore, the new man must be renewed in believers.

Like a growing plant the new nature must be tended and nourished. This happens as believers use the means by which God created the new nature, the means of grace, the gospel in word and sacrament. Through diligent and faithful use of the gospel believers grow in faith and in spiritual knowledge. The more their faith grows, the more it will produce the fruits of loving deeds in their lives. As they experience growth in their faith and their spiritual lives, believers can more effectively defeat the old Adam with its temptations and evil desires. When they arrive in glory, the old nature will be cast off forever and the new nature will be made perfect. In the light of eternal glory believers will finally know God perfectly, even as they are known.

Here on earth there are many distinctions among human beings, and on this basis some people despise and discriminate against others. In verse 11 Paul mentions some of the distinctions that existed in his day. The Greeks considered themselves a particularly cultured and enlightened race, advanced in learning and the wisdom of this world. All who did not share their learning and culture they looked down upon as barbarians. The Jews, God's Old Testament covenant people, took pride in their descent from Abraham and despised members of other races as "Gentile dogs." The Judaizers regarded those who were circumcised as somehow spiritually superior to those who were not. Even the barbarians, those who in that Greek-dominated culture were not schooled in the Greek language, could still look down on the Scythians, a savage, warlike people who were considered culturally the "lowest of the low." And, of course, those who were free could look down on those who were slaves.

Those distinctions, and many more, were maintained in first century society. Similar distinctions, some subtle, some not so subtle, are still maintained in every society in the world. These outward distinctions in human society are not necessarily removed by the gospel. Even after the gospel enters human hearts, some people are cultured and learned in earthly wisdom, others are not. Human beings have different talents and abilities and achieve different levels of earthly success. Differences of race and sex, nationality and color remain. But before God all are sinners, no matter what their earthly differences may be. Jesus died for all, and all who believe in Jesus as their Savior are forgiven and justified, regardless of race, color, rank or social standing.

All who are brought to Jesus have within them that marvelous new nature, which daily grows in knowledge through the gospel, and which enables believers to put off the sins of their old nature and to bring forth the fruits of faith in lives of Christian love. The culture and the learning of the Greek cannot save him. The Jews' descent from Abraham cannot save him. Circumcision cannot save the Judaizer, nor does lack of culture condemn the Scythian or lack of freedom the slave.

Christ saves Jew and Greek, circumcised and uncircumcised, barbarian and Scythian, slave and free. The fullness of all spiritual blessings is found in him, and he transmits his fullness to all his believers. God's grace in Christ Jesus knows no barriers. It bridges all chasms. It makes no distinctions. That grace belongs to us, and we should make no distinctions in sharing it.

Our lives as Christians, then, involve a living and a dying. We live to Christ, with our hearts set on things above, and we die to sin. We put off our old, inherited, sinful nature and put on the new nature which is daily renewed in knowledge and the image of God. May our lives be constantly nourished by the gospel and marked by a continual growing in faith. Then our conscious, concerned and continuing living to Christ and dying to sin will show that we belong to Christ.

12Therefore, as God's chosen people, holy and dearly loved, clothe yourselves with compassion, kindness, humility, gentleness and patience. 13Bear with each other and forgive whatever grievances you may have against one another. Forgive as the Lord forgave you. 14And over all these virtues put on love, which binds them all together in perfect unity.

15Let the peace of Christ rule in your hearts, since as members of one body you were called to peace. And be thankful. 16Let the

173

**word of Christ dwell in you richly as you teach and admonish one
another with all wisdom, and as you sing psalms, hymns and
spiritual songs with gratitude in your hearts to God. [17]And whatever you do, whether in word or deed, do it all in the name of the
Lord Jesus, giving thanks to God the Father through him.**

A Christian's life ought to break with the old vices and be
filled with Christian virtues. In the previous paragraph the
apostle described the negative, the putting off of the sinful,
corrupt nature for which Christians daily strive. In this
paragraph he presents the positive. He shows what virtues
ought to result in Christians' lives from the putting on of the
new nature that is daily renewed in the image of God, and he
urges Christians to live and grow in these virtues. These
virtues are to become permanent, distinguishing marks of
each Christian's life.

For beauty of style and direct appeal to the heart, this
little section is unsurpassed. It is likewise unsurpassed in
practical value. The author of this volume has found this
section to be a particularly rich source of material for wed-
ding addresses. With wonderful clarity the apostle here sets
forth the general, positive principles which ought to govern
Christians' lives in general and our conduct in Christian
marriage in particular.

By God's grace Christians have been made a special people,
a people who belong to God and are united in fellowship with
Christ. It now behooves them to lead lives that conform to the
fellowship they have with their Savior, to express in their lives
and actions the truth that they belong to Christ. In verse 12
Paul addresses believers with words that remind them what
God has made of them. These titles are applied here to the
Colossian believers, but they describe all believers.

Believers, Paul says, are God's chosen people. From all
eternity God, out of pure grace, chose out of the mass of

sinful humanity those whom he would call to be his children. He carries out that eternal, gracious decree in time by bringing individual sinners to faith in Christ through the gospel. This gracious choice did not rest on any merit or worthiness of any individuals, nor was it a matter of some sinners' being more inclined to believe than others. Since Adam's fall, all human beings by nature are equally sinful and spiritually dead. They are equally unable to save themselves or to respond to the call of the gospel.

In his undeserved and unfathomable love God brings it about that some sinners believe the gospel and are saved. The fact that the Colossians believed in Jesus showed that they were chosen ones of God. The fact that we believe in Jesus provides us with the same comfort, and as we use God's gospel and sacraments to strengthen and nourish our faith, we "make our calling and election sure" (2 Peter 1:10).

The fact that God has chosen believers to be his saved people makes them also "holy and dearly loved." Cleansed by the blood of Christ and delivered from the bondage of sin, believers are God's holy ones. They are set apart for him to be the continual recipients of the blessings of his love and to be renewed daily in his image, so they can live lives that serve him. These designations of honor (chosen people, holy, dearly loved) are the same titles that, in the Old Testament, are applied to the ancient covenant people of Israel. Believers in Jesus, no matter what their nationality, are God's covenant people of the New Testament age. In the blessed spiritual condition to which they have been called they are empowered continually to put off the old nature with its sins and vices and put on the virtues associated with the new nature created and continually renewed by the Holy Spirit through the gospel.

As he did in the previous section when discussing vices of the old nature to be put off, the apostle here presents us with

175

a representative sampling of attitudes and virtues that will affect Christians' conduct toward their fellow human beings. These virtues overlap. One leads into or even includes the next, and they are all held together by love.

Clothe yourselves with compassion, the apostle begins. The *compassion* the apostle calls for is a deep feeling of affection rooted in the love of Christ which fills believers' hearts. Believers extend compassion especially to those who are suffering or in distress.

Kindness is somewhat broader than compassion. The very opposite of malice, it is a cordial, loving disposition which knows no harshness. Kindness is shown by believers to anyone whom they can benefit in any way. The early Christians were well known for their kindness, both to one another and to all their fellow human beings. Christians today should also excel in this fruit of faith.

The believer who, with a loving heart, is kind to others does not have too high an estimate of himself. He is clothed with *humility*, the virtue that leads Christians to strive to place themselves below others and to put the welfare of others before their own. Paul is not speaking here of a pretended humility, like that of the false teachers (see chapter 2:18), but of a genuine humility that marks the believer who recognizes his own sin and unworthiness and truly appreciates what God has done for him and for all sinners in Christ. The humble Christian seeks in self-sacrificing love to serve God and the neighbor.

Lowliness and humility were attitudes thoroughly despised by the pagan world. The world today, too, admires assertiveness, self-confidence and pride. "Nice guys," the world tells us, "finish last." But lowliness and self-sacrificing humility were characteristics of Jesus, and he wants those whom he has called into his family of believers to imitate his humility (see also Philippians 2:5-8 and the comments there). By his own humility Jesus ennobled the virtue of humility for his followers. What a happy, peaceful atmosphere exists in a Christian congregation where each member counts the other as better than himself and rejoices to serve others.

The virtue of *gentleness* has also been ennobled by Jesus through his perfect example. Christian gentleness is not a spinelessness that bows before every breeze or refuses to take a stand on any principle. The Christian who follows Jesus will always stand firm in him. At the same time, that Christian will exhibit gentleness in his dealings with others, including his enemies. He will not be easily provoked to fits of rage or anger by the carelessness of others, and he will overlook insults in the spirit of forgiveness. A gentle Christian would rather suffer injury than inflict it.

Together with gentleness the apostle couples *patience*, a "holding out" despite provocation and injustice. The patient Christian does not bear a grudge and refuses to harbor thoughts of revenge when he is wronged. Gentleness and patience are rare characteristics among human beings, but they ought to be distinguishing marks of the chosen, holy and beloved children of God.

As they live together with one another and with their unbelieving neighbors in the world, believers must always remember that they are sinners living with sinners. In spite of all their efforts, there will be lapses in their Christian living. Blemishes and faults will show. There will be occasions when even Christians will hurt each other and complaints against one another will arise. But day after day believers will work to understand. They will *bear with each other* and help each other, lovingly overlooking slights and injuries. They will try to help each other grow, and they will strengthen each other rather than cruelly tearing each other down. And they will cheerfully *forgive each other*, just as Christ has forgiven them.

While he was here on earth, Jesus often encouraged his disciples to cultivate a forgiving spirit. He taught them to pray, "Forgive us our trespasses, as we forgive those who trespass against us." He forgave his enemies from the cross, and on that cross he endured injustice that makes the injuries we may suffer at each other's hands seem minor indeed. Even now, though we often spurn his love, he daily restores and forgives us.

If we understand that, there should never be any question in our hearts about willingness to forgive each other. Think of how the quality of our Christian lives could be changed for the better if all of us learned from the heart to forgive one another — and, having forgiven, to forget. When Paul encourages mutual forgiveness, he is not speaking of a forgiveness with conditions. It is easy to agree to forgive when pardon is asked or amends are offered to soothe our wounded pride, but Jesus' forgiveness to us is not based on any conditions we must fulfill in order to be forgiven. The forgiveness we give to one another should not be, either. Immediate, unconditional forgiveness is forgiveness according to the spirit of Christ. Such forgiveness extinguishes quarrels at their source and refuses to allow resentment or hatred to fester and grow. Is that the kind of forgiveness we are showing in our lives? If it is not, let's ask our Savior's help in doing so.

Over all these virtues, Paul concludes, put on *love*, which binds these virtues all together in perfect unity. Love is the virtue that heads the list of the fruits of faith. It is the crowning virtue in every Christian's life, the one without which all the others cannot even exist. Love, as Paul uses the term here, has a depth of meaning that non-Christians cannot grasp. To a believer love is more than the outward fascination or erotic feelings in which the world glories. It is also much more than the love of mere friendship.

The love which crowns all Christian virtues finds its perfect example in Christ. It is love of conscious, purposeful self-giving that is shown to others, not for the sake of reward, but simply for its own sake. It is love extended even to the unloving and the unloveable, without discrimination. Believers show this love to one another, but it also overflows the boundaries of the Christian community to all their fellow men. This special Christian love in believers' hearts gives value to everything else they do, and it enables believers to move forward together as they strive for the goal of perfect maturity in their lives, a goal they will, by God's grace, ultimately reach in the glory of eternal life.

By emphasizing the importance of love and all the virtues which flow from it and which it binds together, the apostle reminds his readers once more that it is not philosophy or human wisdom or strict outward obedience to regulations and laws, but the love in believers' hearts that leads them forward to maturity and real fullness in their Christian lives. Love, as well as all the other virtues that it binds together, comes alone from Christ, in whom all fullness dwells.

Believers whose hearts are filled to overflowing with love and its fruits will know the Savior's *peace*. Indeed, that peace will rule in their hearts. The peace of Christ is the rest and contentment that fills the hearts of those who know Jesus and his forgiving love. It is the serene feeling that comes from knowing that our sins are forgiven and that we are God's children, that God is our friend and all is well with us. It is the confidence that now and in the unknown future our Savior, who loves us, will work all things for the good of his forgiven children. This peace passes all understanding. It is bestowed on believers by the Spirit through the gospel. As it fills believers' hearts, it enables them to be at peace, not just with God, but also with themselves and with one another.

The word picture in Paul's encouragement to let peace "rule" in believers' hearts is that of an umpire or a referee at an athletic contest. What confusion there would be at such events without officials who understand the rules of the game and make their judgments and decisions on the basis of those rules. With peace as the referee in their hearts Christians will make decisions and carry out actions which promote peace. When divergent claims are made on them, they will let peace be the referee and choose those things which reflect and promote peace among their fellow men. In hearts ruled by peace there will be no room for greed or discontent or jealousy or strife. This will be true among Christians above all, since, when they were called to be believers, they were united with Christ in the fellowship of faith and called to live together in peace.

In the light of what the apostle says here, don't the quarrels, resentments and jealousies that often disrupt peace in our individual and congregational lives seem petty and foolish and totally unnecessary? Are we allowing hatred and discontent over anything to fester in our hearts right now? If we are, let peace be the referee to resolve these conflicts. Let us enjoy to the fullest and reflect to the uttermost the peace that is ours because Jesus won our peace and called us to peace.

Christians whose hearts are filled with Christ's love and ruled by his peace will naturally be *thankful*. Five times in this relatively brief epistle Paul encourages Christians to be thankful. As believers' knowledge of Christ and the spiritual blessings they have in him grow and mature, so will their gratitude, and that gratitude will become evident in their whole manner of living. Love and peace always result in gratitude, and gratitude, in turn, promotes love and peace.

All human beings should give thanks. Christians can be expected to do so. Ingratitude is a mark of paganism. Perhaps it also marked the false teachers who were trying to worm their way into the Colossian congregation. Believers, however, who find their fullness and sufficiency in Christ, ought not to be marked by ingratitude or gloominess, but by joyful thanksgiving. Such a spirit reflects their blessedness and makes them a blessing to others. Does our manner of living reflect the joyful gratitude we have in our Savior?

The new nature in believers and the virtues it produces are the products of the Holy Spirit's work in believers' hearts through the gospel. In order to stand firm and grow in these virtues Christians need to maintain continual contact with the gospel of Christ. That is why the apostle goes on to urge the Colossian Christians to let the word of Christ dwell in them richly in all wisdom. For the Colossians the word of Christ included the Old Testament Scriptures, as well as those inspired New Testament Scriptures which they already had in their possession. For us it includes the entire Old and New Testaments.

The Scriptures, Paul teaches, should be more than something believers hear periodically or invite as an occasional guest into their homes. The word of Christ should inhabit Christians continually, filling every corner of their lives with its blessed spiritual wisdom. Daily Bible study ought to be part of every Christian's life, the hub around which Christian family life revolves.

The Scriptures should also be the focal point of congregational worship and all its other activities. On the basis of the word of Christ and the divine wisdom it imparts, Christians are to teach and admonish each other in public and in private. When the word inhabits them, Christians will grow in faith and knowledge and Christian living, and they will be able to encourage one another. When Christians ignore the Scriptures or use them infrequently and carelessly, they deprive themselves and their fellow believers of blessings which the Lord would gladly shower upon them.

Lives inhabited by the word of Christ will also be lives which overflow with his praise. Paul recognizes the value of Christ-glorifying singing when he encourages believers to sing psalms and hymns and spiritual songs with gratitude in their hearts to the Lord. Martin Luther obviously caught the spirit the apostle here intends to convey when he spoke of music as "a lovely gift . . . which is a precious, worthy and costly treasure given mankind by God."

It is not easy to distinguish sharply between the three terms for believers' songs that the apostle employs here. There may well be some overlapping in meaning. "Psalms" probably refers to the Old Testament book of Psalms, which has served as a hymnbook for both Old and New Testament believers. "Hymns" could possibly be New Testament songs of praise, including inspired hymns like the *Magnificat* (Luke 1) and songs of praise penned by men and women of faith in that early New Testament age. Some Bible scholars think that there may be quotations from early Christian hymns interspersed throughout Paul's epistles, especially in the sections where he bursts forth in jubilant praise to God. "Spiritual songs" are thought to be uninspired sacred songs that are somewhat more subjective in nature. We cannot determine whether these are precisely the distinctions Paul intended or not. It is clear, however, that Paul is reminding believers that we have a rich store of worship resources at our disposal and that we should use those resources to give expression to our gratitude for the blessings of God's grace in our lives.

Nor should believers' singing or any part of their worship be a matter of the lips only. It should be a matter of the heart offered in cheerful spirit to the thanks and praise of God. Scripture does not tell us how many of the things we enjoy here on earth will be present in heaven. It does tell us, though, that there will be singing in heaven. Our homes and churches become forecourts of heaven when we believers raise our voices in Christ-glorifying, man-edifying songs of praise and thanks to God.

Finally Paul summarizes and concludes this whole priceless section by stating the fundamental principle that ought to govern every Christian's life. Whatever you do, he says, do it all in the name of Jesus, giving thanks to God the Father through him. The name of Jesus includes his whole revelation of himself in his word. To do something in the name of Jesus means to do it in vital relationship to him, in harmony with his will, in dependence on his power. Christians do everything in the name of Jesus when they allow their relationship to Christ to control their relationship with everyone and everything else.

Paul fittingly brings this inspiring section to a close with one more reminder to the Colossians and to all of us of the great theme of the entire epistle: Jesus, the all-sufficient Savior. May that Savior, and that Savior only, be all-sufficient for our Christian lives.

The All-Sufficient Christ Sanctifies
Our Family Relationships

18Wives, submit to your husbands, as is fitting in the Lord.

19Husbands, love your wives and do not be harsh with them.

20Children, obey your parents in everything, for this pleases the Lord.

21Fathers, do not embitter your children, or they will become discouraged.

22Slaves, obey your earthly masters in everything; and do it, not only when their eye is on you and to win their favor, but with sincerity of heart and reverence for the Lord. 23Whatever you do, work at it with all your heart, as working for the Lord, not for men, 24since you know that you will receive an inheritance from the Lord as a reward. It is the Lord Christ you are serving.

25 **Anyone who does wrong will be repaid for his wrong, and there is not favoritism.**

4 **Masters, provide your slaves with what is right and fair, because you know that you also have a Master in heaven.**

Whether in the public eye or in the privacy of their homes, Christians are to "do all in the name of Jesus, giving thanks to God the Father through him." Here Paul applies that general principle to believers' family relationships. Later on, in chapter 4:5,6, he applies it to their relationships to their unbelieving neighbors. The result is a kind of "house table" or "table of duties." In the writings of some non-Christian philosophers we also find codes of behavior and suggestions of duties for human society, but only in the Scriptures do Christians find "Do it all in the name of Jesus" written above all our daily duties. Only in Jesus, who stands at the heart of Scripture, do we find the source of love and spiritual strength that will give us the desire and the ability faithfully to fulfill those duties.

The apostle begins his table of Christian family duties by discussing the first and basic family relationship, the relationship between husband and wife. Marriage, of course, is not limited to Christians. It is God's answer to a basic and universal human need. Through marriage God graciously provides the special, intimate companionship that human beings need. He likewise provides for the chastity of man and woman and for the continuation of the human race through the blessing of children.

Marriage is not the same for everyone. The apostle's command to "Do it all in the name of Jesus" raises Christian marriage to a higher level. Nor is the contrast between Christian and non-Christian marriage only an external one. It is not just a matter of less quarreling, bickering or unfaithfulness, though it should certainly include those things.

Doing everything in Jesus' name affects the whole relationship between husband and wife, as their Christian values and attitudes are continually reflected in the way they speak to each other and treat each other.

With remarkable brevity Paul describes the roles that God has assigned to husbands and wives in a Christian marriage. "Wives," he says, "submit to your husbands, as is fitting in the Lord." Modern feminism screams at the word "submit." Women's liberation labels the Apostle Paul a chauvinist and denounces his words as throwback to a less enlightened age. Words like submit and obey, they tell us, must be removed from the marriage ceremony, and what they imply must be removed from the marriage. The feminist movement, however, cannot eliminate this passage from the Scripture. It cannot eliminate what Scripture consistently teaches about this subject. Nor does it take the time to try to understand what Scripture is really saying here.

As we consider this passage, it is well for us to remember that it is not only the Apostle Paul who is speaking here, it is the Lord. We should not forget either that what the apostle says here to wives is only half of a total picture. All the apostle's instructions in this section are reciprocal, and the full significance of what Paul is saying here to wives emerges only after we study his corresponding instructions to husbands. Most important of all, we must never forget that all the instructions in this section are given in the spirit of genuine love.

So what does the apostle mean when he urges Christian wives to be submissive to their husbands? He does not mean that the woman is inferior. In heathen cultures women have been and, in some places, still are regarded as inferior, but Christianity gives dignity to women. This same Apostle Paul tells us in Galatians 3:28 that in Christ, that is, with regard to salvation, there are no distinctions between male

185

and female. Paul's call to Christian wives to be submissive, however, reminds us that insofar as this life is concerned, God created man and woman different, both biologically and emotionally.

He created the man first, then the woman to complement the man, to be a "suitable helper" for him. This order of creation is reflected in the family relationship when the husband is recognized as the head, the leader of the family. If you try to create something with two heads, or with no head, you end up with a monster. God makes it clear that in a marriage relationship the greatest blessings occur when the Christian wife willingly acknowledges her husband's leadership and acknowledges it for the best possible reason, because it is "fitting in the Lord."

As we have already stated, all of the apostle's instructions in this family duties section are reciprocal. We cannot understand the full significance of what he is teaching unless we study both parts of his instructions. The counterpart to "Wives, submit to your husbands" is NOT "Husbands, lord it over your wives," but "Husbands, love your wives and do not be harsh with them." To no husband does the Lord give the right to be a tyrant or dictator in the home.

A Christian husband's treatment of his wife is to reflect kindness, consideration, gentleness, dignity and a steady, unwavering love, a love similar to the Savior's love for his believers. This love, true Christian love, willingly gives and sacrifices without expecting anything in return. It is strange, is it not, that some husbands seem to take it for granted that their wives will help them with their work but refuse to lift a finger to lighten their wives' domestic load? The love the Lord calls for in Christian husbands does not take that attitude. It is always gentle and considerate, never demanding or harsh.

Nor does the fact that the husband is the God-appointed head of the family mean that he will make the family decisions arbitrarily or unilaterally. The husband who seeks to be an effective head of his family will take time to communicate with his wife. He will seek out her counsel, try to understand her feelings and seek to discuss family issues and problems in a reasonable, open, loving way. Together husband and wife will go to God's word for its advice regarding decisions that confront them and affect their family life. Together they will pray for wisdom and sound Christian judgment in matters not directly addressed by God's word. And the whole sordid matter of a husband's physical abuse of his wife should not even have to be mentioned among Christians.

In Ephesians, which in many respects is a companion epistle to Colossians, Paul compares the relationship that ought to exist between a Christian husband and wife to that which exists between the Lord and his church. As unthinkable as it would be for Christ to turn against the church, to be harsh with it or mistreat it in any way, so unthinkable should it be for a Christian husband to mistreat his wife or to be harsh with her. As the church joyfully responds to Christ's love with willing service, so wives should willingly submit to their husbands' leadership as it is fitting in the Lord. A Christian husband's love will make his wife's submissive role, not a galling or distasteful thing, but a reciprocal expression of self-giving Christian love.

The American family is in trouble today. Each year close to a million families are broken up. Who of us has gone through a year in the last decade without observing the breakup of a family somewhere in the circle of our relatives and friends? Is there a reader of this volume who has not felt strains in one form or another on his own family relationships?

Our society lacks respect for the institution of marriage and disregards the role that God assigns to husbands, wives and children. This has contributed greatly to the sad condition of family life in our nation. There are, of course, no perfect marriages here on earth, because there are no perfect people. But as Christ's love fills the hearts of Christian husbands and wives and they follow his directions, as each one seeks to love and serve the other, they will build marriages and homes that will stem society's tide, marriages that will last and homes in which peace and happiness will prevail because God's blessing rests on them.

Next the apostle speaks about the relationship between children and parents. Children are to obey their parents in everything. God gives parents responsibility for their children and authority over them. Under God parents are responsible for the physical, emotional, mental, social and spiritual development of their children. As they carry out their responsibilities, parents dare not let the children do just as they please. That would be a grave disservice to them. Rather, parents are to require obedience of their children, and children are to render that obedience, not just when parents ask them to do what is easy and pleasant, but also in those things that are difficult or tedious. Christian children are to obey, not grudgingly or with a grumbling spirit, but willingly, knowing that, in the final analysis, they are obeying not just their parents but the Lord.

Such willing obedience pleases the Lord. That is why in both the Old Testament and the New he attaches to the Fourth Commandment, "Honor your father and your mother," the encouraging promise, "that it may be well with you and that you may enjoy long life on the earth." One of the best ways children can show their love for God is by obeying their parents. God promises to parents who require obedience and to children who give it the blessings of a quiet, peaceful and happy home.

God wants parents to require obedience of their children, but Scripture and experience teach that obedience does not come naturally. Obedience has to be taught. At times it has to be insisted upon through correction and discipline, even with the rod of corporal punishment, but God has a word for parents here, too. Parents are not to discourage their children or make it difficult for them to obey. Rather they are to prove themselves worthy of their children's respect and obedience. As they teach their children obedience, parents must not be inconsistent, dictatorial, unreasonable or harsh.

God does not want parents to be permissive and give their children everything they want, nor does he want them to be so harsh with their children that they become bitter or get the feeling that they cannot do anything right or pleasing to their parents. Children's spirits are fragile and can easily be broken. Discipline should never be a parent's way of taking his frustration and anger out on the child. It should always be the result of the parent's loving desire to teach the child to avoid the wrong and follow the right way. God wants parents to love their children, and both fathers and mothers should not be ashamed to verbalize and display that love. There's much to be said for the sentiment expressed by the bumper sticker slogan, "Have you hugged your kid today?"

What a beautiful thing it is when Christian parents create in their homes a warm and loving atmosphere in which children find joy in obedience. On the other hand, what untold tragedies have resulted when parents, even though they may have truly loved their children, have embittered the children through lack of proper direction and discipline, excessive harshness or failure to properly and effectively communicate their love.

Parents who love their children will also take care to nourish their children's spiritual lives. Not just mothers, but

189

fathers, too, will take a personal interest in their children's spiritual training. In families where fathers, as well as mothers, attend worship services with their children, the children are much more likely to worship regularly when they are on their own. Above all, Christian parents will provide an example that will make God's word live for their children.

Child-rearing in our society is a difficult and often discouraging task. The sinful nature of both children and parents, as well as the multitude of temptations with which the devil seeks to lead children and adolescents away from the path of loving obedience, at times threatens to overwhelm Christian parents. But if both parents and children seek the Lord's help and follow his instructions, they can become more obedient children and more understanding parents. Nor should parents, even in the most discouraging moments of their child-rearing experiences, stop trusting in the Lord's encouraging promise in Proverbs 22:6, "Train a child in the way he should go, and when he is old he will not turn from it."

In Paul's day slaves, too, were part of the family relationship. The mighty Roman empire ran on slave power. It is estimated that at one time perhaps a third of the empire's population consisted of slaves. Convicts or prisoners of war were made slaves. Others were kidnapped by slave traders and forced into slavery or became slaves because they could not pay their debts. Children of slaves, of course, were also considered slaves.

Paul here speaks of slaves as belonging to their masters' households, because many slaves lived and worked in their masters' homes. Light manufacturing was done in homes. The master or the lady of the household would supervise anywhere from two or three to several dozen slaves in producing textiles, pottery, jewels, shoes and other saleable items.

As the Christian gospel proceeded throughout the empire, many slaves became Christians. Occasionally their masters did, too. In either case it posed a question: How could the child of God, master or slave, relate his new religious status to his social standing? Paul addresses that question in what some might consider to be a surprising way. Although in 1 Timothy 1:10 he condemns slave traders as immoral, he does not advocate, here or elsewhere, the immediate abolition of slavery. He does not call on masters to free their slaves or on slaves to revolt against their masters. Immediate abolition of slavery would bring chaos to the empire, and it would cause much human suffering, especially to those who were slaves. The violent overthrow of society's institutions is not the Christian way. Many social reformers today miss a key point that the apostle makes here, namely, that the gospel aims primarily, not at changing social patterns, but at changing hearts. The apostle took social structures as he found them and spoke with the gospel to those who lived in them. If changes in the structures and institutions of society resulted from changes worked by the gospel in human hearts, those changes evolved quietly and peacefully. The apostle's instructions to slaves and masters, if followed, would eliminate the evils and brutality associated with slavery and would dignify the labors of Christian slaves, both in their own eyes and in the eyes of their masters.

To Christian slaves Paul simply says, "Obey your earthly masters in everything." The only exception to such obedience would be a master's command that was contrary to God's will. Christian slaves should not be obedient simply to catch the master's eye or impress him when he happens to be watching. They should obey with genuine sincerity. If those who served would only remember that ultimately they were serving Christ, they would find dignity and nobility in even the lowliest task. Laziness, dishonesty and ill will toward their masters would be replaced by integrity, honesty and willing service.

By wholehearted cooperation and full obedience to their masters, Christian slaves would also be promoting the cause of Christ. Their masters would see what transforming power the gospel has in hearts and lives. Even though those dutiful Christian slaves might never be properly rewarded for their efforts here on earth, the Lord himself assures them that, in the eternal inheritance that he has prepared for them, he will recognize and graciously reward the service they rendered to their earthly masters as part of what they did for him. On the other hand, both slaves and masters are reminded that the Lord sees how they treat one another. Those who deliberately do evil, no matter what kind of excuse they might think they have, will find that the Lord will not lightly overlook their misdeeds.

Paul's directions to masters likewise emphasize mutual kindness and love. According to Roman law a slave was a piece of property without any rights. A master could buy, sell, even kill a slave legally. There were grotesque evils associated with slavery. Paul calls on Christian masters to exercise their lordship in the name of Jesus. Christian masters are to treat their slaves humanely, never forgetting that they, too, are answerable to a master, one much greater than themselves. They were answerable to the heavenly Master, who died to save both slaves and free. The souls of all, no matter what their social standing, are precious in his sight, and he can fill the hearts of both slaves and free people with his love and enable both to live their lives to his glory. In an application of Jesus' golden rule to the slave/master relationship, the apostle urges Christian masters in Colosse to treat their slaves in exactly the way they would want to be treated by the heavenly Master.

Paul has more to say in these verses about the slave/ master relationship than about any of the other family relationships. This was only natural, because with this letter and the epistle to Philemon the apostle was sending a runaway slave, Onesimus, back to his master, Philemon, in Colosse. Onesimus is mentioned in verse 9 of this chapter, and the entire Epistle to Philemon, also included in this volume, is addressed to this situation.

The Christian principles that Paul sets forth for the relationship between Christian slaves and masters can provide guidelines for modern Christians in employer/employee relationships. Through these words of the apostle the Lord gives dignity to our work. As Christians we serve the Lord with our faithful and diligent labor in our various earthly callings. Our daily labors are the fruits of our faith and ought to be carried out in the spirit of serving the Lord. Throw yourself into your work, the apostle would urge today's Christian laborers, as if your employer were the Lord.

Here on earth the employee who works diligently at his task may never be rewarded or earn any more than fellow employees who just "put in their time." He may, at times, even become the object of his peers' ridicule. But the Lord sees the fruitful labor of all his believers. Above all he sees the attitude of their hearts, and he will graciously acknowledge and reward their faithfulness when they enter their heavenly home.

The Lord would likewise have employers deal fairly with their employees. Employers, too, have a master in heaven. If employers and employees followed these simple guidelines and respected each other in unselfish Christian love, many of today's difficulties between labor and management would disappear. As a blessed byproduct, the nation's economy, based not on greed but on mutual consideration, would flourish. May each Christian employer and employee who reads Paul's inspired directives to the Colossians remember that, though we may not be able to change the world, we can, with the Lord's help, begin to change our little corner of it, as we carry out all our tasks diligently and faithfully, doing them all in the name of Jesus.

The All-Sufficient Christ Enables Us to Live Lives of Prayer and Wisdom

²Devote yourselves to prayer, being watchful and thankful. ³And pray for us, too, that God may open a door for our message, so that we may proclaim the mystery of Christ, for which I am in chains. ⁴Pray that I may proclaim it clearly, as I should. ⁵Be wise in the way you act toward outsiders; make the most of every opportunity. ⁶Let your conversation be always full of grace, seasoned with salt, so that you may know how to answer everyone.

The word of God establishes true peace in believers' hearts and moves them to live at peace with one another. Closely connected with the word, and arising out of its command and promise, is yet another aspect of Christian living, believers' prayer lives. In the word of God, specifically the word of the gospel, the hand of God reaches down to sinful men. In prayer, the hand of man, encouraged and empowered by the word, reaches upward to God.

If love is the firstfruit of faith, prayer is its heartbeat. Countless times throughout the Scriptures the Lord urges believers to come to him in prayer. He wants us to bring before him all our wants and needs of body and soul, as well as those of our fellow believers. He wants us to pray even for our enemies. He wants us to pray to confess our sins and to praise and thank him for his goodness, and he promises to hear and answer every believing prayer.

With all that in mind Paul simply says, "Devote your-selves to prayer." As we pray, we Christians are to be watch-ful and thankful. We are to be alert to the needs that God wants us to bring to him and awake and sincere when we bring them. We are to be alert to the dangers and tempta-tions all around us that threaten our faith and require our prayers. We are to be conscious of the blessings we have received from the Lord and thankful for them.

The Apostle Paul has a special request to make of the Colossians with regard to their prayers. He asks that they remember him, together with Timothy, Epaphras and all those laboring together with him for the cause of the gospel. When he asks for the Colossians' prayers, however, Paul does not ask prayers for the benefit of his own person, not even prayers for his release from prison. Paul's chief concern is for the cause of the gospel. So he asks the Colossians to pray that God might open a door for the gospel message and continue to bless the preaching of the gospel and its ad-vancement in the world, and he asks them to pray that the Lord would continue to give him the wisdom and the cour-age faithfully and effectively to proclaim the gospel mes-sage.

If we assume, as many do, that Paul's epistle to the Colossians was written before the epistle to the Philippians, Paul may well have been thinking here of his imminent appearance before the imperial court. What an unparalleled opportunity that court appearance would give the apostle to proclaim the good news of Christ before the highest officials of the empire. Obviously, the apostle must have been an effective speaker. Yet he asks his fellow believers to continue praying that his testimony to the gospel would be effective and easy for people to grasp.

When a good message is proclaimed in a bad way, its effect may be lost. Paul asks for the Colossians' prayers that his human limitations and fears might not get in the way of a clear and powerful proclamation of the gospel to the visitors, both Jews and Gentiles, who came to him at Rome, to the Roman soldiers who guarded him and the Roman officials who would hear his case. Philippians 1:10 indicates that the prayers of the Christians on Paul's behalf were favorably answered. In that passage Paul informs his readers that it has become clear throughout the city that he is not preaching some illegal or unpatriotic religion, as his Jewish enemies have charged. Through his clear and courageous testimony, many new converts, including some soldiers and government officials, have been won for Christ.

When we offer our prayers, our Lord does not want us to be thinking only of ourselves, of "us four, and no more." He wants us to remember our government, our fellow believers, the members of our congregation, the sick and the dying, the erring, all those in need of special comfort and help. He also wants us to remember our pastors and teachers and the missionaries who proclaim the gospel for us throughout the world.

When was the last time you prayed for your pastor? Have you perhaps criticized him more recently than you have prayed for him? What a powerful aid to its success a congregation has when more and more of its members pray, together with their pastor, that the Lord might enable him to grow in his understanding of the word and in his ability to communicate that precious message from the pulpit and in the classroom, to young and old, to the troubled and the sick, the dying and the bereaved.

Any number of missionaries have told us that they are convinced that it is only through the prayers of the Christians "back home" that they are blessed with the special strength they need to fulfill their often difficult and dangerous calling. Some of the most cherished encouragement I have ever received in my personal ministry came from a kind and concerned "matriarch" of a large family in my congregation who, before the Lord took her to her eternal home, assured me frequently, "Pastor, our family is praying for you." Pray for us, dear readers, that we may proclaim the mystery of Christ clearly, as we should.

The Colossians were to pray for the success of the gospel. Their conduct should also serve the gospel's cause. Paul concludes this final series of admonitions with a word about Christians' relationship to unbelievers, or, as he terms them here, outsiders. In the spirit of doing everything in the name of Jesus, Paul urges Christians to be wise in the way they act toward unbelievers.

In the days of the early church Christians were often viciously slandered by those outside the church. Non-Christians accused them of being atheists, because they served an unseen God, and of being unpatriotic, because they refused to burn incense to the emperor. The best way for Christians to defeat such slander, Paul says, is by wise conduct. The reputation of the gospel depends to a large extent on the conduct of those who claim to believe it. People may not read the Bible, but they read Christians.

Christian wisdom will lead believers in their daily conduct to avoid anything that might prejudice outsiders against the gospel. Indeed, the positive testimony of believers' service to the Lord and to their fellow men might well touch the consciences of some outsiders and help win them for Christ. The most effective way for Christians to advertise the gospel is to conduct themselves in a way that will make it evident that Christ's love has filled their hearts and lives.

Not only is living wisely important for Christians. There is also an urgency about it. Do not put off advertising the gospel with your lives, the apostle pleads, but make the most

197

of every opportunity. The days are evil. The battle is difficult, and the Lord is coming soon.

Believers' testimony to the world, not just their speaking about Jesus, but their speaking about everything else as well, should be full of grace, seasoned with salt. Gracious speaking is speaking that imparts grace to those who hear it. Such speaking is not necessarily conversation dotted with witty or clever remarks. It is conversation that results from the operation of God's grace in our hearts. "Seasoned with salt" refers to the wholesomeness of what we say. Salt is a preservative; it prevents decay. And it makes food more tasty. "Seasoned speech" coming from the mouths of Christians is speech that Paul describes in Ephesians as "not corrupt, but useful."

A Christian's speech should be marked, not by the foul and improper language that is so characteristic of worldly society, but by language that is distinctively Christian, language patterned after the gracious speaking of Christ. For that kind of speaking the Lord has placed us Christians on earth. The most important kind of speaking Christians can do is the speaking they do on behalf of their Savior, explaining their Christian conduct and testifying of their heavenly hope.

It takes a great deal of tact and wisdom for Christians to live in such a way that their entire behavior and all their speaking glorify God and give to outsiders a positive testimony to the gospel. With the encouragements with which he closes this section on Christian living the apostle would ask each of us to look closely at his life in the world. Can the fact that we belong to Jesus be seen by others, especially by others outside the Christian faith, as they observe our lives and listen to our conversations? Do the lives we live and words we speak sparkle with the love of Jesus and our joyful commitment to him? Or have we been so thoroughly influenced by the world around us that we could easily pass for worldly-minded people?

Throughout this entire epistle the apostle has, in a lofty and eloquent manner, pointed us to the all-sufficiency of Jesus for our salvation and our Christian living. May his sufficiency continue to fill us with the desire and the ability to glorify him with our speech and our lives, so that our whole being may give evidence of the wondrous life and sure hope we have in him.

Greetings and Conclusion

[7]Tychicus will tell you all the news about me. He is a dear brother, a faithful minister and fellow servant in the Lord. [8]I am sending him to you for the express purpose that you may know about our circumstances and that he may encourage your hearts. [9]He is coming with Onesimus our faithful and dear brother, who is one of you. They will tell you everything that is happening here.

[10]My fellow prisoner Aristarchus sends you his greetings as does Mark, the cousin of Barnabas. (You have received instructions about him; if he comes to you, welcome him.) [11]Jesus, who is called Justus, also sends greetings. These are the only Jews among my fellow workers for the kingdom of God, and they have proved a comfort to me. [12]Epaphras, who is one of you and a servant of Christ Jesus, sends greetings. He is always wrestling in prayer for you, that you may stand firm in all the will of God, mature and fully assured. [13]I vouch for him that he is working hard for you and for those at Laodicea and Hierapolis. [14]Our dear friend Luke, the doctor, and Demas send greetings. [15]Give my greetings to the brothers at Laodicea, and to Nympha and the church in her house.

[16]After this letter has been read to you, see that it is also read in the church of the Laodiceans and that you in turn read the letter from Laodicea.

[17]Tell Archippus: "See to it that you complete the work you have received in the Lord."

¹⁸I, Paul, write this greeting in my own hand. Remember my chains. Grace be with you.

The apostle now brings his epistle to a close with an introduction of the messenger who is bringing the letter to its destination, final greetings from his associates to the Colossians and personal greetings to various members of the congregation. It is a special feature of this epistle that Paul mentions a rather large number of fellow Christians and co-workers. Only here and in the last chapter of Romans does he send such extensive greetings.

Here nine names are mentioned, including seven men with whom Paul was in contact during his imprisonment. By studying these verses we can discover a little more about the men that surrounded the apostle during the difficult, yet productive days of his imprisonment. We can also gain a little insight into the intimate and cordial spirit that prevailed among all the Christians and particularly among those who labored together for the cause of the gospel in the early days of the church.

Timothy was with Paul when he wrote this epistle, but he is not mentioned here because he is mentioned in 1:1, together with Paul, as a sender of the letter. The first of Paul's co-workers named in this section is Tychicus, no doubt because it was he who carried this letter, together with the apostle's letters to the Ephesians and to Philemon, to their destinations. Tychicus was one of Paul's closest friends and most valued allies. He was a native of the province of Asia and, quite likely, of the city of Ephesus. He had accompanied Paul to Jerusalem when the apostle delivered the collection that the believers from the outlying areas had taken for the needy in that city. Later he spent time with Paul in Rome during the apostle's imprisonment.

Tychicus receives high praise from Paul. He is called a "beloved brother, a faithful minister, a fellow servant of the

Lord." Because he had recently been with Paul, Tychicus was an ideal messenger to supply the Colossians with information about how Paul was faring in his imprisonment. He could also provide any other personal information they might desire about Paul, his associates or any other of their Christian acquaintances in Rome. This epistle contains very little personal information about Paul, the conditions of his imprisonment or the prospects of his court hearing. Here the apostle tells us the reason. Some things are better spoken than written. Paul wants Tychicus personally to supply the Colossians with the latest information about his imprisonment and court case, including any developments that might take place in the short time between Paul's completion of his letter and Tychicus' departure for Colosse. Though they may never have met Paul personally, the Colossians were concerned about his welfare. Paul appreciated that concern and made this arrangement to keep them informed.

There was another reason, too, that Paul sent one of his most trusted assistants to Colosse. He wanted Tychicus to "encourage your hearts." Remember, the Colossians and their faith were under siege. The false teachers, with their philosophical Christianity, were threatening to make inroads into the congregation. As a personal representative of the Apostle Paul and a competent and faithful servant of the Lord, Tychicus could add also his encouragement to that provided by the apostle in the letter. That would give the Colossians a double source of strength to stand firmly on Christ and the gospel.

Accompanying Tychicus would be Onesimus. We shall speak at length about Onesimus in the commentary on the book of Philemon. To sum it up briefly, Onesimus was a slave who had escaped from his master Philemon in Colosse and fled to Rome. In Rome he met the Apostle Paul, learned the gospel and became a Christian. Now Paul was sending him back to his master under the protection of Tychicus. Tychicus also carried a personal letter to Philemon, urging Philemon to forgive Onesimus and receive him back, not just as a returning slave, but as a fellow believer.

Here Paul commends Onesimus to the entire congregation, underscoring to them what he has personally written to Philemon. By permitting Onesimus to stand with Tychicus as an informant concerning his affairs, the apostle visibly demonstrates to the congregation that he regards the converted Onesimus as a faithful and dear brother. Onesimus was one of them, not just in a physical sense because he was a native of their city, but one of them in spirit, a fellow believer in Jesus.

In verses 10-14 Paul's three companions of Jewish birth (Aristarchus, Mark, Jesus Justus) and three of Gentile birth (Epaphras, Luke, Demas) send greetings to the Colossians. They, too, are concerned about the Colossians' spiritual welfare. They want the believers in Colosse to know this, and they want them to know that they concur with everything the apostle has written.

Aristarchus was a Jewish native of Thessalonica. On Paul's third mission journey he was with the apostle at Ephesus, where he was seized by the angry crowd of idolaters. His name is also mentioned in Acts 20, Luke's account of the return leg of the journey. Aristarchus probably accompanied Paul on his perilous journey to Rome and worked with the apostle during at least part of Paul's imprisonment in the imperial capital. Paul calls him a fellow prisoner, not because he, too, is on trial, but because he is someone who has volunteered to be with Paul and to assist him during the apostle's imprisonment.

Mark, also known as John Mark, authored the second of the four Gospels. Paul mentions that he was a cousin of Barnabas, since some of the Colossian Christians must have met Barnabas on one of Paul's stops during his first mission journey. On that journey Mark had accompanied Paul and Barnabas part of the way, but then had turned back. Because of this, Paul refused to take Mark along on the second journey. This led to a sharp disagreement between Barnabas and Paul and resulted in their parting. By the time Paul wrote these words, however, Mark had nobly redeemed himself. The apostle no longer regarded him as a liability but commended him warmly as one who had been a comfort to him. That this relationship continued is clear from the fact that Paul also praises Mark in 2 Timothy, his last epistle.

What brought about the change in Mark and his relationship to the apostle? Undoubtedly Mark had matured, both emotionally and spiritually. Perhaps Paul's discipline had sobered him. Maybe Barnabas, or even Peter, with whom Mark is also frequently associated, had taken him under his wing and tutored him. Peter certainly knew what it meant to fall and be lifted up again. Whatever the reason for the change, we now remember Mark, not as the man who deserted the apostle, but as the man who came back, and we admire him for it.

As Paul wrote these words about him, Mark was apparently ready to undertake an assignment that would bring him into the general area of Colosse. Perhaps Paul had given him that assignment. Maybe it was a task he was doing for Peter or Barnabas. At any rate, the Colossians already knew about this visit of Mark and had received instructions about it. To those previous instructions Paul added an encouragement to the Colossians to receive this faithful servant when he came to them, to show him hospitality and provide for his physical needs. Incidentally, the fact that Paul had forgiven Mark, who had once forsaken him, was certainly a silent encouragement to Philemon to forgive his slave Onesimus, who had once forsaken him but was now returning to him.

The name of Jesus Justus, another Christian of Jewish background, is otherwise unknown to us. Both names were rather common among Jews in the Roman empire. This is the only mention of this man that Paul ever makes, but the report concerning him is favorable. Of all the Jews, including the Jewish Christians in Rome, these three were the fellow workers that gave the apostle real comfort.

There is disappointment in Paul's words here. For the most part, the members of his own race had disowned the apostle. Romans 9:1-5 is a further commentary on Paul's love for the Jews and his deep sorrow in their rejection of Jesus and the gospel. Perhaps certain Jewish Christians in Rome were among those who preached Christ, but had no love for the apostle (see Philippians 1:15-18). These factors must also have served to intensify Paul's feelings of appreciation for the service that these faithful three were rendering to him.

Next follow greetings from three of Paul's companions of Gentile origin: Epaphras, Luke and Demas. We have heard of Epaphras in the introduction to Colossians and in chapter 1:7, where Paul speaks warmly of the man and his work of proclaiming the gospel in Colosse, Laodicea and Hierapolis. Epaphras had apparently founded all three of these congregation in the Lycus Valley. This faithful servant of Christ, out of genuine concern for the Colossians' spiritual welfare, brought Paul the report that prompted him to write this epistle. Epaphras sends his regards to the Colossians.

Paul also wanted the Colossians to know that Epaphas was praying for them. As a regular part of his daily routine Epaphras, who was perhaps the one person most aware of the spiritual dangers facing the Colossians, wrestled in prayer with the Lord on the Colossians' behalf. Daily he prayed that the Lord would give them strength to grow and mature in their faith and help them give expression to that faith in their lives. Daily he prayed that the Colossians would be able to meet and successfully combat all the spiritual dangers they were facing.

The fact that Epaphras sent his greetings, while Tychicus was returning to Colossee with Paul's letter, seems to imply that Epaphras was not planning to return to Colosse at once, but would remain for a while with the apostle in Rome. Perhaps he wished to study with Paul or to lend assistance to his "ministry in chains." Paul's warm commendation of Epaphras for a second time in this brief epistle reminded the Colossians that, despite the attempts of the gospel's enemies to demean him, Epaphras had been a faithful servant of the Lord in Colosse. The Colossians should be loyal to Epaphras and the gospel he proclaimed, not to the "learned" new teachers.

Most of us are familiar with Luke. A Gentile Christian who traveled extensively with Paul, Luke too was noted for his faithfulness. He was an educated man, a "beloved physician," universally loved and admired by the Christians of his day. He was the inspired author of both the Gospel that bears his name and the book of Acts. The New Testament sketches we have of him portray him as a remarkable person: always near the Apostle Paul and the gospel, always faithful to both. Among the apostle's last recorded remarks in 2 Timothy is the telling observation, "Only Luke is with me." Luke and Paul were kindred spirits. Both were educated, sympathetic, committed and faithful to the gospel's cause.

The last of Paul's associates to greet the Colossians has a less honorable history. Demas would one day prove to be a great disappointment to Paul. During the apostle's second and last imprisonment he would write, "Demas, because he loved this world, deserted me" (2 Timothy 4:10). Did Paul already see signs of that fatal weakness when he wrote these words to the Colossians? We don't know. But the fact that in the close circle of Paul's associates there was someone who proved to be unfaithful, just as there was one traitor among Jesus' twelve disciples, is certainly a warning against over-confidence to every Christian.

The apostle wanted certain greetings to be forwarded by the Colossians to believing neighbors. He wanted the church at Laodicea, the neighboring congregation with which the Colossian Christians were closely associated, to be greeted. In connection with the greeting to the Laodiceans Paul singled out a woman named Nympha and the church in her house for a special, personal greeting. Who was Nympha, and why did she and the church in her house receive special greetings? We can only speculate. Perhaps a group of Christians in Laodicea who lived close to each other, but were separated by a rather inconvenient distance from the rest of the Christians there, met at Nympha's house, or maybe a smaller group of Christians in the third city of the Lycus Valley triangle, Hierapolis, met at the house of Nympha.

It was customary in the days of the early church for apostolic letters to be circulated among the churches. The apostle asks that that be done with this letter. After it had been delivered to the elders of the Colossian congregation it would, of course, be read to the assembled Colossian church. From the Colossians his letter was to be passed to the believers in Laodicea. They were facing the same problems the Colossians were. So the letter would also be beneficial for them.

Now, however, comes a difficulty. Paul says that the letter from the Laodiceans should also be read in the Colossians' midst. There is, of course, no letter to the Laodiceans in our New Testament. To what, therefore, is the apostle referring?

Of all the explanations that have been suggested to solve this mystery of the missing letter, two seem to stand out as the most reasonable. Perhaps there was an epistle to the Laodiceans, but it has been lost. We know that at least one letter of the Apostle Paul was not preserved for posterity (1 Corinthians 5:9). Perhaps there were others. We do know that severe earthquakes rocked the area around Colosse shortly after Paul's letters were sent to the region. The destruction they caused may well have resulted in the loss of even the most carefully kept manuscript.

Another possibility is that the letter from the Laodiceans may actually have been the letter we know as Paul's epistle to the Ephesians. Along with the epistle to the Colossians and that to Philemon, the epistle to the Ephesians was carried by Tychicus. If the letter to the Ephesians was passed along a more or less regular circuit, it would naturally have come from Laodicea to Colosse. Both theories about the letter to the Laodiceans seem possible, although they are only speculation.

Verse 17 is crisp and abrupt. It contains instructions to Archippus, who was a member of Philemon's family, probably his son. To this young man Paul simply says, "See to it that you complete the work you have received in the Lord." Some see a rebuke in these words and conclude that Archippus may have fallen behind in some project the apostle or the congregation had assigned to him. This is possible, but not likely. If Archippus had been lazy or disorganized, why would Paul honor him with the title "fellow soldier" in Philemon 2? It is more likely that Paul's instructions to Archippus here are similiar to those he gave Timothy (2 Timothy 4:5): "Discharge all the duties of your ministry."

207

The fact that Paul calls Archippus a "fellow soldier" seems to indicate that Archippus, like Paul, was serving as a minister of the gospel. That would mean that he was the pastor serving the Colossian congregation while Epaphras was away at Rome. Paul's words would then be words of encouragement to that young "vacancy pastor," words confirming and supporting the call and the ministry of a relatively inexperienced pastor facing a difficult task. With his encouragement to Archippus Paul was also tactfully encouraging the congregation to support this pastor and cooperate with him.

It was customary for the apostle to close his letters by writing a few words with his own hand. He did this both to mark the letter as genuine and to discourage the forged letters that were appearing with claims to be apostolic. As he closes, Paul again refers to the fact that he is a prisoner for the sake of the gospel. This gives him a right to expect the Colossians to listen to what he has to say to them. With this reminder he also again asks for their prayers, and he challenges them, too, to be willing to suffer for the gospel.

With a short benediction, "Grace be with you," Paul brings his epistle to a close. Those four little words, especially in view of all Paul has previously written in this epistle, say much to the Colossians and to us. Grace, God's undeserved love in Christ, is the basic blessing that Christians possess and cherish. It transforms human hearts and lives and leads believers onward to glory. Grace is the basis for faith and the power for Christian lives. The word ought ever to remind Christians that they are saved, not by their own wisdom, efforts or strength, but only as a result of God's undeserved love in Christ. Wisdom, discernment, strength, victory over temptation, and all Christian virtues are the products of grace. That marvelous grace of God in Christ Paul pronounces on the believers in Colosse as he brings his epistle to a close, once more holding before them the wondrous blessings that are theirs in the all-sufficient Christ.

PHILEMON
INTRODUCTION

Only four of St. Paul's thirteen epistles (1 and 2 Timothy, Titus and Philemon) are addressed to individuals. Of these four, Philemon is easily the most personal. Yes, there is a greeting for the church of believers that met at Philemon's house, but the letter contains no other general instruction or advice for the church as such. Rather it is a personal and very touching appeal from Paul, the apostle and Christian gentleman, to Philemon, the church leader and likewise a Christian gentleman.

Although various other lessons can be found in what the apostle has to say and the manner in which he says it, the letter revolves around one major item of business: a special request from Paul to Philemon regarding a runaway slave whom Paul was sending back to Colosse from Rome. That personal nature of this epistle is precisely what makes it special. This often forgotten epistle is also God's inspired word. That makes it worth our study.

C. S. Lewis called Philemon, "the most beautiful and intensely human of all St. Paul's epistles, full of charm and beauty." Others have described it as the "most gentlemanly letter ever written." Anyone who takes just a few minutes to read through the single chapter of this 25-verse epistle will be both impressed and moved by it. It deserves more attention than its small size might indicate. Perhaps this little volume can increase our appreciation of this unpretentious letter.

Although separated from it by five other epistles in our present arrangement of New Testament books, Paul's epistle to Philemon is a very natural companion to his letter to the Colossians. Philemon and Colossians were written at the same time and sent to the same destination with the same messenger. In Colossians there are references to the individuals mentioned in Philemon, and the third chapter of Colossians encourages the spirit of forgiving love that the apostle urges on Philemon in particular. This is why our editors have chosen to place Philemon in this particular volume of *The People's Bible*, even though at first glance it might seem "out of order."

The epistle to Philemon was addressed to an individual Christian in Colosse. We know very little about this man. Paul addresses him from his imprisonment as "dear friend and fellow worker." We gather from the letter itself that Philemon must have been converted to Christianity by Paul, either directly or indirectly. Perhaps Philemon had received personal instruction from the apostle in Ephesus, or perhaps he had been one of those in Colosse who had been brought to faith through the ministry of Paul's pupil, Epaphras, who founded the congregation in Colosse. In any case Philemon became a very active member of the Colossian congregation. He opened his home for the worship services of the mission congregation. He established a reputation among his fellow Christians as a generous, loving, hospitable believer and in general a devoted worker for the Lord and for his church.

Paul's greeting to Philemon also includes the names of Apphia, who is generally assumed to be Philemon's wife, and Archippus, who was probably Philemon's son. Both Archippus, who was apparently serving as the pastor of the Colossian congregation at the time this epistle was written, and Onesimus, the subject of the epistle, are mentioned in Colossians chapter 4. Apphia and Philemon are not. Everything we know about the man whose name is attached to this New Testament epistle is found within the epistle itself.

211

The reason Paul wrote this personal letter to Philemon was to intercede with his Christian friend for a man named Onesimus. Onesimus (the name means "profitable") had previously been a slave in Philemon's household. But Onesimus had run away, probably with his pockets lined with money he had stolen from his master. Eventually, as many escaped slaves did, Onesimus made his way to Rome. There he providentially came into contact with the Apostle Paul. Paul, we recall, was under house arrest in the city, awaiting the outcome of his appeal to the imperial court. The apostle, who during his imprisonment "welcomed all those who came to him," welcomed also this rather disreputable character. Even more significantly, he instructed Onesimus in the gospel.

As the Lord had blessed Paul's ministry to the master, so he blessed it to the slave. Onesimus became a Christian. A warm, personal bond quickly developed between the apostle and the converted slave, whom Paul calls "my son" in Philemon 10. Onesimus' new faith and his deep personal loyalty to the apostle quickly became evident in his actions. In the past Onesimus had been unprofitable and thus untrue to his name. Now he began living up to that name. By his grateful, devoted service to the apostle as the imprisoned apostle's "legs" in Rome, Onesimus endeared himself to Paul and served the cause of the gospel well.

Paul no doubt would have liked to keep the newly profitable Onesimus with him in Rome. He probably could have prevailed on Philemon to allow him to do so, but the apostle felt that this course of action was not a decision, or even a proper suggestion, for him to make. He honored all of society's ties and was well aware of the 10th Commandment and its warning against covetousness.

He does not command or plead with Philemon to set Onesimus free. The purpose of the gospel is not to change the social order, but to change human hearts. Paul was confident that the gospel in the hearts of both masters and slaves would result in the elimination of slavery's abuses and lead slaves and masters to a new respect and Christian concern for one another. So Paul sent him back to Philemon. He went under the protection of another co-worker, Tychicus, and he went willingly. He went to seek his master's forgiveness and a return to his service.

But how would Philemon react to the return of the slave who had been so unprofitable to him? Under Roman law a master had the legal right to inflict severe punishment, even death, on a runaway slave. So Paul sent a personal letter with Onesimus and Tychicus. We know this letter as the epistle to Philemon. In this letter the apostle tactfully and lovingly intercedes with Philemon on Onesimus' behalf. He pleads with Philemon, who is well known in the Christian community for the practice of Christian love, not to treat Onesimus with the harshness and cruelty so typical of that age. He urges him, instead, to show the forgiving spirit that marks those who are truly followers of Jesus.

In making his appeal, the apostle speaks to the heart of Philemon. He refers to Onesimus, not as an unprofitable runaway, but as his child in the faith. He assures Philemon that, by virtue of his conversion, Onesimus is no longer just a slave, although the master/slave relationship still exists. Onesimus is now also Philemon's Christian brother. Paul offers to pay Philemon out of his own pocket for any damage or financial loss he might have incurred because of Onesimus' unfaithfulness. In the same breath, however, the apostle reminds Philemon that he himself owes Paul an inestimable debt, for he became a Christian through Paul's ministry.

We can measure the strength of the bond between Paul and Philemon by the confidence with which the apostle makes his request. One can hardly imagine that Philemon would do anything less than honor the apostle's tactful request, forgive his penitent runaway, and welcome him back. The fact that this epistle still exists argues that he did.

There are no great doctrines set forth in this short epistle. Only one sermon text from Philemon is even suggested in the major text series used by most pastors. Yet the twenty-five verses of this little epistle offer us some valuable spiritual lessons. They show us, first of all, that there is no line of cleavage between Paul the apostle and Paul the man. The motto of both is, "To me, to live is Christ" (Philippians 1:21). This entire epistle breathes the loving, forgiving spirit of Christ and the Christian view of things that ought to be evident even in what might seem to some to be the insignificant matters of life.

Paul's plea for Onesimus is a model Christian intercession. As such, it mirrors the intercession of Christ for us. "We are Christ's Onesimi," Luther remarked, "restored by Christ, who, by giving up his rights, compelled the Father to lay aside his wrath." This epistle is also a marvelous example of Christian tact. Its tone and structure are well suited to encourage Philemon's generous nature and to touch his very heart. Christians do well to imitate the apostle's example of tactful love as they deal with and appeal to one another.

Outline of Philemon

Theme: A Model Intercession

Greeting and Thanksgiving (1-7)
I. Paul's Plea for Onesimus (8-21)
II. Other Related Matters; Farewell and Benediction (22-25)

GREETING AND THANKSGIVING
PHILEMON 1-7

1 Paul, a prisoner of Christ Jesus, and Timothy our brother,
To Philemon our dear friend and fellow worker, [2]to Apphia
our sister, to Archippus our fellow soldier and to the church that
meets in your home:
[3]Grace to you and peace from God our Father and the Lord
Jesus Christ.

[4]I always thank my God as I remember you in my prayers,
[5]because I hear about your faith in the Lord Jesus and your love
for all the saints. [6]I pray that you may be active in sharing your
faith, so that you will have a full understanding of every good
thing we have in Christ. [7]Your love has given me great joy and
encouragement, because you, brother, have refreshed the hearts
of the saints.

As he addresses Philemon, both here and later in the body
of this epistle, Paul emphasizes, not his apostolic authority,
but the fact that he is a prisoner for the gospel's sake. It is a
prisoner, but certainly not an ordinary prisoner, who sends
Philemon this special plea. Paul calls himself a prisoner of
Christ Jesus. The apostle rightly regards his imprisonment,
not as a disgrace, but as a badge of honor, because it resulted
from his faithful service to the Lord. He is confident that all
the details of this imprisonment, as well as its final outcome,
are in the hands of the Lord, who governs the whole universe
in the interest of his church. Paul's reference to his imprisonment for Christ's sake both here and again in verse 9 is
certainly also part of his tactful appeal to Philemon.

Philemon was to understand that the special request of this letter was coming to him from one so deeply committed to the cause of Christ that he had surrendered his very freedom for it. How could Philemon refuse to honor such a request? Philemon might reflect on the fact that, though he was outwardly a free man, he was not necessarily free to do what he pleased. As a servant of Christ he was free to do what was right. Timothy, Paul's associate and the brother in faith of both Philemon and the apostle, joins Paul in sending greetings. He agrees with all that Paul is about to say to Philemon in his brother to brother request.

Paul calls Philemon "our dear friend and fellow worker." Love for the Lord Jesus joined Paul, Philemon, Timothy and the whole family of believers together in a special union. On the basis of that love Paul will make the appeal of this epistle. He is confident that Philemon will respond on the basis of that same love. By calling him a "fellow worker" Paul refers favorably to the manner in which Philemon has given evidence of his faith, especially among his fellow believers. Some of the specific ways in which he did that will be mentioned later, especially in verses 5-7. It is sufficient to note here that Paul addresses Philemon respectfully, as an active lay leader of the church, a man who according to his ability worked for the cause of the gospel. Still today, the efforts of believers like Philemon help the visible Christian church to survive and to flourish.

"Apphia our sister" and "Archippus, our fellow soldier" are so closely associated with Philemon that the apostle mentions them in the same greeting. The inference here seems to be that Philemon is the head of the family to which Apphia and Archippus also belong. It is generally assumed that Apphia was Philemon's wife. Archippus was probably their son.

The encouragement that Paul gives to Archippus in Colossians 4:17 seems to indicate that Archippus was the pastor in charge of the Colossian congregation, at least during the time that Epaphras was in Rome with Paul. Paul addresses him here as a fellow soldier, a companion in arms who stands together with the apostle in the forefront of the battle against sin and the forces of the devil.

Philemon, of course, is the person to whom this letter is first of all directed. It is he, and only he, who will have to decide on the matter Paul sets before him, but Paul wants those who are close to Philemon to hear the letter too, so that they can encourage Philemon to decide on a God-pleasing course of action. Paul also wants them all to have their Christian knowledge increased and their spirit of forgiveness broadened.

Finally, Paul also greets the church that meets in Philemon's house. In the first and second centuries church buildings were practically non-existent. Families would usually hold worship services in their homes for their own households. Those who had larger homes would often invite other families to join them in their worship. Mary, the mother of John Mark, did this in Jerusalem (Acts 12:12); Lydia did it in Philippi. Philemon seems to have had a large house which he offered as a place of worship for the believers in Colosse. This was one of the many ways in which Philemon made his love for the Lord and his fellow believers evident. Paul acknowledges that here, and then takes the opportunity to extend greetings to all who gather for worship in Philemon's house.

The greeting in this epistle is Paul's familiar "Grace and peace." On Philemon, Apphia, Archippus and the members of the Colossian congregation Paul pronounces God's forgiving love. He reminds them that the love of God in action, Christ's substitutionary death for a world of sinners, brings sinners peace of heart and conscience, because through Jesus' blood they are reconciled to God. These basic and vital spiritual blessings have their source in God the Father and in the Lord Jesus. It is to one who he knows has been deeply affected and greatly blessed by God's grace and peace that Paul addresses this epistle with its special appeal. The apostle is confident that God's grace and the peace, with which God's forgiving love has filled Philemon's heart, will move him to show the same kind of forgiving love to the penitent Onesimus.

According to his usual custom Paul follows his greeting with a thanksgiving and a prayer. Whenever Paul thought of Philemon or remembered him in his prayers, there was much for which he gave thanks. Epaphras, the founder of the Colossian congregation, who was now with Paul in Rome, as well as others, including the newly converted Onesimus, must have told Paul about Philemon's exemplary faith and Christian life. Philemon's commitment to Christ and his energetic work for the Lord's cause, together with his love for his fellow Christians, were well known in and beyond the Colossian congregation. He had opened his home for the worship services of the congregation, given help to the less fortunate and made valuable physical and spiritual contributions to the welfare of the Christian community in Colosse.

The apostle's approving mention of these evidences of Philemon's faith was not just insincere flattery. It was honest praise. Paul no doubt intended it to serve another purpose as well. By reminding Philemon of the many ways in which his faith had already shown itself in love, the apostle wanted to prepare his Christian friend for the great request of this epistle, a request to carry Christian love one step farther than ever before by forgiving and receiving back the slave who had so severely wronged him.

Paul tactfully prepares Philemon for that great request. He also prays that the Lord will strengthen Philemon's love at its source by strengthening his faith and enabling him to share and give evidence of that faith. Christians possess incomparable spiritual treasures in Christ. The more they are aware of those treasures and recognize the good things that are theirs in Christ, the more active they will be in promoting and sharing their faith and in reflecting the Savior's love in their lives by adopting a loving, forgiving attitude toward others. Paul's prayer is that the Holy Spirit, who has filled Philemon's heart with faith and enabled him to give so many practical evidences of that faith in the past, will continue, through word and sacrament, to bless him with growth in spiritual understanding. Such growth, in turn, would lead to ever greater evidences of faith and love in Philemon's life and enable him to perform the special act of love which Paul is about to request of him.

Philemon was not a stranger to faith's firstfruit. In the past, Paul says, Philemon's love had often refreshed his weary fellow believers. Reports of his love had often filled the apostle's heart with encouragement and joy. Now Paul will appeal to the man he regards as a true brother in the Lord Jesus to refresh his fellow believers once more and to bring joy to the imprisoned apostle's heart by lavishing the full measure of his mature Christian love on a returning runaway slave.

We can hardly imagine a greater example of Christian tact than the inspired apostle shows here as he prepares Philemon for his special request. What an impressive reminder the apostle's words are for all of us. Our lives as Christians, too, should be a constant growing in the faith and subsequent love that will enable us to take more and ever greater steps of love, as we deal with one another and with all our fellow human beings.

PAUL'S PLEA FOR ONESIMUS

PHILEMON 8-21

⁸Therefore, although in Christ I could be bold and order you to do what you ought to do, ⁹yet I appeal to you on the basis of love. I then, as Paul — an old man and now also a prisoner of Christ Jesus — ¹⁰I appeal to you for my son Onesimus, who became my son while I was in chains. ¹¹Formerly he was useless to you, but now he has become useful both to you and to me.

¹²I am sending him — who is my very heart — back to you. ¹³I would have liked to keep him with me so that he could take your place in helping me while I am in chains for the gospel. ¹⁴But I did not want to do anything without your consent, so that any favor you do will be spontaneous and not forced. ¹⁵Perhaps the reason he was separated from you for a little while was that you might have him back for good — ¹⁶no longer as a slave, but better than a slave, as a dear brother. He is very dear to me but even dearer to you, both as a man and as a brother in the Lord.

¹⁷So if you consider me a partner, welcome him as you would welcome me. ¹⁸If he has done you any wrong or owes you anything, charge it to me. ¹⁹I, Paul am writing this with my own hand. I will pay it back — not to mention that you owe me your very self. ²⁰I do wish, brother, that I may have some benefit from you in the Lord; refresh my heart in Christ. ²¹Confident of your obedience, I write to you, knowing that you will do even more than I ask.

With verse 8 the apostle begins to discuss directly the primary business of this letter. His plea to Philemon on Onesimus' behalf is a model intercession, for it is based solely on Christian love. In the previous verses Paul laid the foundation for an appeal to Philemon's heart. Now he makes that appeal in a direct and forthright manner. Paul was the Lord's apostle. As an apostle Paul had special authority in the church. Had he chosen to use that authority, he might simply have commanded Philemon to do what he was about to request. In this case, however, Paul did not want to do it that way. He did not want to lay this request on Philemon as an obligation or a duty. He wanted it to be a matter of love. So he set himself before Philemon, not as an apostle with authority, but as an old man and a prisoner of Jesus Christ, who is appealing to Philemon's love.

According to our standards Paul was not really very old. He was probably in his sixties, but life expectancy in the first century was not as great as it is now. Paul had no doubt grown old beyond his years because of the many hardships and deprivations he had experienced in his service of and suffering for the gospel. Even as he wrote these words Paul was imprisoned for the gospel's sake. Philemon loved and respected the apostle. As a Christian who customarily showed love to others, he would find it hard indeed to refuse a special appeal to love from the beloved apostle.

We twentieth-century Christians can learn much from the manner in which the apostle makes his appeal here. We live in a society in which demands are more common than appeals. Assertiveness, we are told, not tact, gets people ahead in life today. The apostle here shows us the better way. The most powerful motivating force on earth is not intimidation or threat or assertion of what one perceives as one's own rights, but love. That is true to an even greater degree among Christians, whose love finds its motive and example in Jesus' self-giving love for us. On the basis of that love Jesus constantly intercedes for us with the Father. The most effective appeals from one Christian to another and even, in a more limited way, from Christians to non-Christians, will be those based on love.

Paul chooses his words very carefully. As a faithful intercessor, he places himself between the one for whom and the one with whom he is pleading as he makes the request for which this epistle was really written. With tender affection and beautiful tact, calling the runaway slave "my son" and the one "who became my son while I was in chains," Paul brings the subject of Onesimus directly before Philemon.

Using a play on words involving the slave's name, he describes the wonderful change the Lord has brought about in Onesimus' heart and life. Onesimus, a rather common slave's name, means "profitable" or "useful." Formerly, of course, Onesimus had been untrue to his name. He had been a runaway and a thief, particularly unprofitable to Philemon. Perhaps Philemon cringed at the very mention of the name Onesimus. But now, Paul informs Philemon, the Onesimus who has been instructed in the gospel and converted to Christianity has become truly useful. He has already been useful to Paul, and he will again be useful to Philemon, if only Philemon will receive him. Paul further describes the deep affection that has grown up between him and Onesimus. He is confident that such affection could quickly grow up also between Philemon and Onesimus when he tells Philemon, "I am sending him — who is my very heart — back to you."

Paul was sending Onesimus back to Philemon, and Onesimus was willingly returning to the master he had wronged, because both were convinced that this was the proper, Christian course of action. After his conversion Onesimus had become a loyal friend and helper of the imprisoned apostle. He has assisted Paul with his apostolic labors, probably serving as the imprisoned apostle's messenger and personal servant. In fact, Onesimus had been so helpful to him that the thought had crossed Paul's mind more than once that he should keep Onesimus with him. Paul could even credit Onesimus' service to Philemon, he reasoned, because the apostle was sure that Philemon wanted to do something to help him during his imprisonment, but was prevented by distance from doing so. How could Philemon have refused such a request from the apostle, if he had made it?

But Paul knew that it would not be proper for him to presume on Philemon's generosity in that way. He did not want to put Philemon in a situation in which a generous gesture would be forced on him, rather than flowing spontaneously from a loving heart. So, as far as Paul was concerned, there was only one thing to do. He would send Onesimus back to Philemon. If Philemon then wanted to do something more, perhaps even send Onesimus back to the apostle "on loan" until Paul was released from his imprisonment, that decision would be entirely Philemon's.

As he sends Onesimus back to Philemon, Paul makes no attempt to excuse the past behavior of the slave who has been unprofitable. As he encourages Philemon to forgive and receive Onesimus, however, the apostle asks the master to note the various ways in which the Lord has overruled the wrong Onesimus has done and made it serve for good.

Onesimus had been brought into contact with Paul and been converted to Christianity. Paul had gained a devoted Christian friend and a helper for his ministry. There was a definite possibility that, in the end, this whole affair would bring good to Philemon, too. When Onesimus had run away, Philemon had been deprived of a slave and his service. He had suffered loss for a time. Now, if he received Onesimus back, Philemon would have him back permanently, and he would have him back in a new and infinitely better relationship. As a Christian slave Onesimus would serve Philemon in a much more joyful and efficient manner than he had ever served before. He would now be doing his work for Philemon as if he were doing it for the Lord.

In addition, Philemon and Onesimus would now share a precious spiritual bond that they had not shared before, the bond of a common faith. Beyond their physical relationship of slave and master they would share a spiritual relationship as brothers in Christ. This blessed fellowship cuts through all earthly and social ties and continues throughout eternity. At the same time, it sanctifies and changes for the better all earthly relationships.

On the basis of all these things, therefore, Paul summed up his plea: "Welcome him as you would welcome me." Paul knew that, if he himself were to come to Philemon, his friend would gladly and hospitably receive him. By faith, Paul, Onesimus and Philemon were now all brothers in Christ. How could one brother in Christ, if he has truly absorbed the spirit of Christ, fail to lovingly receive another brother who came to him in repentance and sought his forgiveness?

There was one other factor that Paul felt should be mentioned, since it posed a potential threat to Philemon's warm reception of Onesimus. That was the financial loss Philemon had suffered as a result of Onesimus' previous actions. While Paul never comes right out and says it, it is quite likely that Onesimus stole money from his master before he left for Rome. There was also the matter of the service of which Philemon had been deprived during the time Onesimus was gone. That, too, could have been valued at a considerable sum.

Paul did not want that factor to stand in the way of Philemon's receiving Onesimus. If Philemon considered it to be a problem, Paul says, he should charge the debt to Paul's account. Paul had become Onesimus' spiritual father. He was ready to assume a father's obligations. Would Paul have been able to come up with a substantial amount of money if Philemon had requested it? We have no way of knowing. What is clear is that Paul was serious about his offer. He wanted absolutely nothing to stand in the way of Philemon's receiving and forgiving Onesimus.

Besides, Paul fully expected Philemon to remember that, when it came to the matter of settling accounts, he owed the apostle something so valuable that it could not be measured by standards of earthly valuation. Philemon owed his spiritual life to Paul. It was either directly through Paul's instruction or indirectly, perhaps through the instruction of Paul's student Epaphras, that Philemon had become a Christian. Wasn't the spiritual benefit he had received from the apostle, Paul tactfully suggests, more than enough to counterbalance the material losses he had suffered because of the unfaithfulness of Onesimus?

A positive response by Philemon, Paul says, would bring him true spiritual refreshment. It would bring the apostle a special measure of spiritual joy to see Philemon put his faith and love into practice in this extraordinary way and to see these two spiritual sons of his reconciled to one another. A positive answer by Philemon to the apostle's request — and Paul was confident that such an answer would be forthcoming — would bring Paul, too, into the blessed circle of those to whom Philemon had given spiritual refreshment by his love. This is always the way it should be among Christians. Those refreshed by the gospel news of love and forgiveness in Christ constantly refresh one another by showing in their lives the loving, forgiving spirit of Christ.

In addition to the marvelous example it gives us of a loving, tactful appeal from one Christian to another, Paul's eloquent intercession for Onesimus in these verses can also be regarded as a reflection of our Savior's loving intercession for us. Like Onesimus, we sinners have all wronged and run away from our heavenly master. We deserve nothing but his wrath and condemnation. But, as Paul found and rescued Onesimus, Jesus has found and rescued us. He stood between the Father and us. He identified himself with us by taking on our nature and becoming our substitute. He not only offered to pay, but did pay our sin-debt on the cross to satisfy divine justice. Now, as our great High Priest, he intercedes for us daily, whenever we sin. The Father cannot refuse to listen to the intercession of his Son or refuse to pardon those who by faith are Christ's brothers and sisters and his own children. "We are Christ's Onesimi," Luther put it, "if you will receive it."

OTHER RELATED MATTERS, FAREWELL AND BENEDICTION

PHILEMON 22-25

22 And one thing more: Prepare a guest room for me, because I hope to be restored to you in answer to your prayers.

23 Epaphras, my fellow prisoner in Christ Jesus, sends you greetings. 24 And so do Mark, Aristarchus, Demas and Luke, my fellow workers.

25 The grace of the Lord Jesus Christ be with your spirit.

Paul does not even have to wait until he hears whether or not Philemon has acted on his request. He is confident that his Christian friend has thoroughly imbibed the spirit of the gospel, and he trusts him to do what is fitting, loving and right. Paul, in fact, is sure that Philemon will find ways of doing even more than what has been requested of him. So, as far as the apostle is concerned, the major matter which prompted the writing of this letter is settled and closed.

There is one more request, however, that Paul has to make of Philemon. The fact that he unhesitatingly makes it is yet another evidence of Paul's confidence that Philemon will honor the intercession of this letter and that this whole incident will result in further cementing the bonds of their friendship. Paul expects to be released from his imprisonment in the near future. After his release, he wants to visit Colosse. During that visit he and the various assistants that traveled with him will need a host and place to stay. Paul asks Philemon to be that host.

Among the first century Christians, when traveling was difficult and there was nothing comparable to our modern motels, hospitality was considered a special virtue. Well-to-do Christians like Philemon frequently "refreshed the saints" by providing necessary accommodations for their fellow believers, like the apostle, when they traveled through or stopped to work in their cities.

That he expects his release from imprisonment to take place rather soon is something the apostle credits to the prayers of his fellow Christians. Paul began this epistle with a reference to prayer. He closes it in much the same way. Not only has the apostle been praying for Philemon and the Colossians. He knows that they have also been praying for him. This is as it should be. Those who share God's grace in the gospel should regularly remember one another before the throne of grace.

The apostle's expected release, a release for which so many Christians had been praying so fervently, would be dramatic evidence once more that God is moved to gracious actions by believers' prayers. All the evidence we have indicates that Paul was released from this particular imprisonment and permitted to make more journeys on behalf of the gospel, and he did use the guest quarters at Philemon's home.

The greetings Paul conveys in this epistle are from five of the men mentioned in Colossians 4:10-14. The reader may wish to review what was said about each in that section. Epaphras is mentioned first, probably because he had been Philemon's pastor at Colosse. Jesus Justus, who is mentioned in Colossians, is not mentioned here, probably because he was not personally known to Philemon.

The fact that these servants of the gospel sent their greetings shows that they, too, had a vital interest in the outcome of this matter. Like Philemon, they were fellow laborers with the Apostle Paul for the cause of the gospel, and all were convinced that the cause of the gospel would be wonderfully served and promoted if Philemon showed his returning slave forgiving love modeled on and motivated by the love of Christ.

Upon Philemon, Apphia, Archippus and all who gathered for worship in their home; yes, on all the Colossian believers and on every believer down through the ages who reads this epistle, Paul, God's apostle, pronounces God's grace. Grace, God's unmerited love for lost and fallen sinners, is his most important gift to sinners, and it is the source of every other spiritual blessing. As it fills believers' hearts through the gospel, it gives birth to a peace beyond human understanding, and it empowers believers to live lives that give evidence of that love.

No one has attached a postscript to this epistle. We have no knowledge of Philemon's reaction to Paul's plea, but a positive inference is inescapable. If Paul was absolutely confident that Philemon would honor his request, why should we not be? The very fact that this letter has been preserved to the church is a silent argument that its eloquent plea fell on a sympathetic ear. May each of us, likewise, be moved by this beautiful little epistle to seek and to practice a faith which, in all circumstances of life, works by love.

SOLI DEO GLORIA

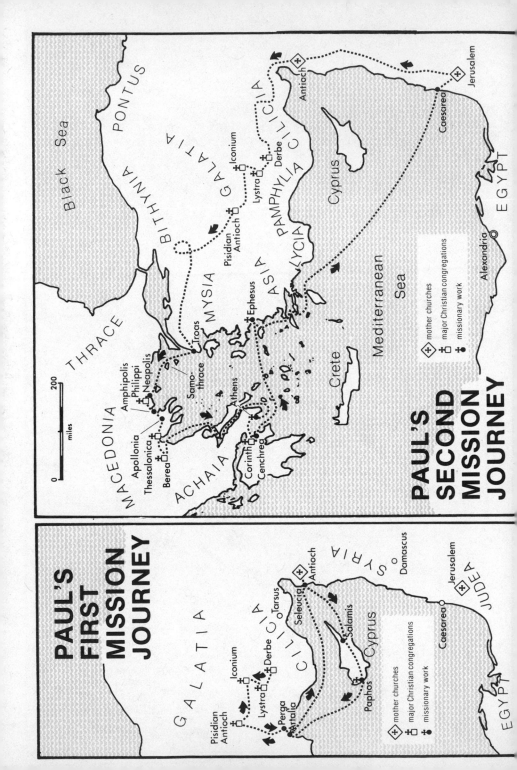

PAUL'S FIRST MISSION JOURNEY

Black Sea

PONTUS

BITHYNIA

GALATIA

Iconium
Pisidian Antioch
Lystra
Derbe
Tarsus
CILICIA

Antioch
Seleucia
SYRIA

Damascus

Perga
Attalia
PAMPHYLIA

Salamis
Cyprus
Paphos

Caesarea
Jerusalem
JUDEA

EGYPT

⊕ mother churches
□ major Christian congregations
✝ missionary work

PAUL'S SECOND MISSION JOURNEY

Black Sea

PONTUS

BITHYNIA
GALATIA

Iconium

Pisidian Antioch
Lystra
Derbe
CILICIA

Antioch
LYCIA
PAMPHYLIA

Cyprus

Alexandria
EGYPT

Caesarea
Jerusalem

ASIA

Ephesus

MYSIA
Troas

THRACE

MACEDONIA
Amphipolis
Philippi
Neapolis
Samo-
thrace
Apollonia
Thessalonica
Berea
ACHAIA
Athens
Corinth
Cenchrea

Crete

Mediterranean
Sea

200
miles
0

⊕ mother churches
□ major Christian congregations
✝ missionary work

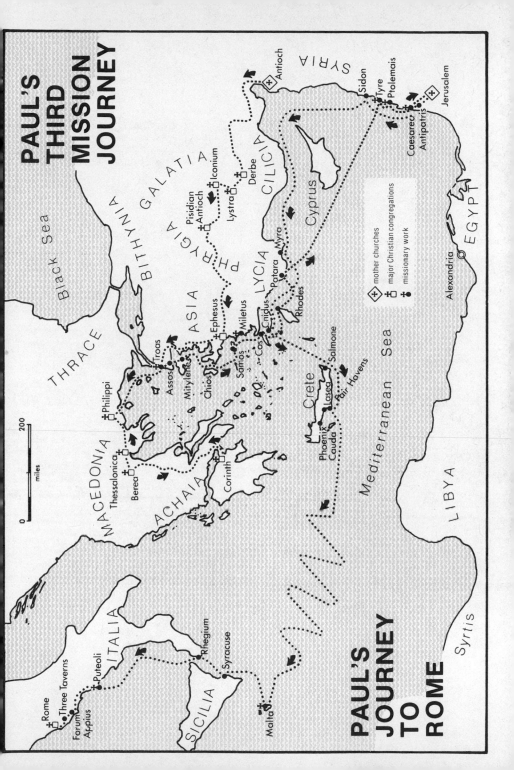

PAUL'S
THIRD
MISSION
JOURNEY

PAUL'S
JOURNEY
TO
ROME

✠ mother churches
✠ major Christian congregations
• missionary work

Black Sea

THRACE

BITHYNIA   GALATIA

PHRYGIA

ASIA

Pisidian
Antioch   Iconium

Lystra   Derbe

LYCIA   CILICIA

Myra

Patara   Cnidus

Rhodes   Cyprus

Troas
Assos
Mitylene
Chios
Samos   Cos

MACEDONIA

Philippi

Thessalonica

Berea

ACHAIA

Corinth

Ephesus
Miletus

Crete
Lasea   Salmone
Phoenix   Fair Havens
Cauda

Mediterranean Sea

LIBYA

Syrtis

EGYPT

Alexandria

SYRIA

Antioch

Sidon
Tyre   Ptolemais
Caesarea   Jerusalem
Antipatris

ITALIA

Rome
Three Taverns
Forum
Appius   Puteoli

Rhegium

SICILIA

Syracuse

Malta

200
miles
0